To Hari —
Keep searching
Keep finding
your
inner
light!

DIGITAL
DHARMA

Steven Vedro
Portland
Oct 27, 07

DIGITAL DHARMA

A User's Guide to Expanding Consciousness in the Infosphere

STEVEN VEDRO

QUEST

BOOKS

Theosophical Publishing House
Wheaton, Illinois • Chennai, India

Quest Books
Theosophical Publishing House
P.O. Box 270
Wheaton, IL 60189-0270

www.questbooks.net

Cover image: Chad Baker/Getty Images
Cover design, book design, and typesetting by Dan Doolin

Library of Congress Cataloging-in-Publication Data

Vedro, Steven.
Digital dharma: a user's guide to expanding consciousness in the infosphere / Steven Vedro.
p. cm.
Includes bibliographical references and index.
ISBN-13: 978-0-8356-0859-6
ISBN-10: 0-8356-0859-X
1. Internet—Moral and ethical aspects.   2. Cyberspace.   3. Self-perception.   4. Internet—Social aspects.   I. Title.
TK5105.878.V43 2007
303.48'3—dc22   2007003340
5   4   3   2   1   *   07   08   09   10

Printed in the United States of America

Contents

ILLUSTRATIONS

Preface

I have always loved the stuff of communications technology. As a child, I was content to sit for hours in front of the big shortwave set in my uncle's living room searching for voices from far away. As a ten-year-old I learned Morse code and as a teenager became involved in pirate radio, regularly ruining the neighborhood TV reception whenever I started my home-brew broadcasts. In college, I spent most of my time at the campus FM station. My summer work as a film projectionist and TV cameraman (I covered home plate at Shea Stadium in New York) paid for much of my tuition. I have produced television programs, designed educational video networks and Internet sites, and helped PBS stations make the transition to digital broadcasting. I'm the kind of techno-aficionado who can enjoy a walk down a country lane gazing at the wildflowers—while also calculating the line loss in the cable TV wires on the poles overhead.

But even in the midst of my technology adventure, I knew something was missing in my approach to life. I began studying meditation, which eventually led me to the study of Sufism, esoteric healing techniques, and the philosophy of tantra, or energy yoga, and its system of network concentration centers called the *chakras*. Suddenly words such as channeling, radiation, and field intensity took on meanings quite different from the technical terms I had mastered years before.

While this new work opened my heart, I was not at peace with the continued separation between my vocation and my spiritual life. I did not want to quit my "day job" as an educational technology consultant; I was too excited about helping schools and public broadcasting stations build new digital networks. On the other hand, the kinds of experiences I was having as a student of energetic healing touched a deeper desire to be of personal service, one heart at a time. I was also bothered by my "more spiritual" friends' reaction to technology. It troubled me that they took pride in disdaining computers and not owning televisions.

I saw no way to bring these two worlds together until I started rereading some of the key books of my college years—the works of Lewis Mumford and Marshall McLuhan on technology and civilization—through the lens of my new teachers: masters such as Sri Aurobindo, the Theosophists, Pierre Teilhard de Chardin, and today's scholars of noetic consciousness, including Michael Talbot, John White, Ken Wilber, Peter Russell, Duane Elgin, Christian de Quincey, and Howard Rheingold.[1] I returned to the field of media ecology that had stimulated me so much in the 1970s and '80s and gobbled up dozens of new books on the social impacts of the Internet, "flash mobs," "small networks," cellphones, and the alphabet itself. Then, one night, I had a defining dream:

> *I have died and am waiting outside Heaven's door. My spiritual guides, long-dead family members, angels, and teachers are gathered to meet me. But I see they're shaking their heads. After a while they approach me. "Steven, Steven," they say gently, "we told you to go work with Light in the world. We didn't expect you to take us so literally!" And in a rapid series of images, I see my life's "energy work" flash in front of me: theatrical lighting designer, stage electrician and spotlight operator, film projectionist, radio transmitter engineer, designer of fiber optics and wireless video networks. All that work, so close, and yet not quite on the mark!*

I woke up troubled. Had I really only heard half the message? Was my entire love for communications all a cosmic misunderstanding? Was I supposed to give up my technology career to start a New Age counseling practice? Was a 900-number "healing line" in my future? No, my work was to try to bring these worlds together by using the metaphors of communications to help make understandable the more arcane teachings I had learned in my energy healing and meditation circles.

I am not a guru or enlightened master. Nor am I an academic. While this book is richly footnoted (offering links to media criticism, spiritual philosophies, and recent news articles), it is not an intellectual treatise but rather a statement of personal wonderment at the connectedness of the inner and outer worlds. In it, I suggest that we look at the media metaphorically, finding encoded in it the same core lessons of human evolution and transformation recalled by all of the world's spiritual traditions. Out there in the "Infosphere," past the wires and optical fibers, the chips and satellites, beyond the debates about media content and the social impacts of technology, there is a lesson for us about how we earthlings must now communicate. I believe that mastering the challenges of the cyber-age can become a step on the evolutionary path of consciousness towards greater self-awareness and enlightenment. Choosing the path of "right conduct" when everyone and everything is electronically connected is now part of our collective spiritual practice—our "digital dharma."

* * * * * *

This book started as a storytelling session at my fiftieth birthday party, in 1998. Sitting at my feet were my many dear friends, and their support has been with me all these years.

Along the way from story to manuscript I received masterly help from my editors Lonny Brown and Jane Andrew and my agent John White. Murray Lennox of the Satir Learning Community of Ottawa and the Inner Focus School reviewed the engineering concepts and the chakra correlations. Musician friend Dr. Molly Scott reviewed the chapter on telephony and analog resonance. Lee Goldberg, editor of analogZone, moved from a former student to a peer teacher. Anodea Judith taught me much about the chakras, and Alexandra Parness and Paul Ditscheit guided me through my apprenticeship as an energy healer. Abraham Sussman initiated me into the Sufi Ruhaniat Order and shared many Sufi tales that have found their way into this manuscript.

Dr. Cynthia Smith, Eric Howland and Julie Shaull, Marilyn Wedberg, Marcia Welch, David and Danielle Devereux-Weber, Rhea Vedro and Graham Yeager, and Bryan and Fanou Walton have commented on various versions of this book or have worked with me as I tried out different "teleconsciousness visualizations" (or both). Philosophers Duane Elgin and Ken Wilber encouraged me along the way; Leonard Shlain has graced me with hours of his time and much elder wisdom. My brother Peter Vedro always recognized that this was more than just a personal tale and set my sights on the big picture. And standing by my side, urging me to "get writing" so that I could really tell this story, has been my soul mate and partner, Dr. Beverly Gordon. Portions of this work have appeared in print in *Technos Quarterly* (Bloomington, IN), *The EDGE Newspaper* (Minneapolis), and *The Beacon: A Journal of Esoteric Philosophy* (London and New York) and on the Web site of Jeremy Gluck's Spiritech Virtual Foundation (now hosted at http://www.geocities.com/spiritechuk/vedro.html).

INTRODUCTION

Dharma is about our spiritual duty to find teachings in all aspects of daily life. Today, our souls are incarnated in bodies that swim in a sea of information. Our media are not outside our life, but are intimate extensions of our being. As extensions, they mirror and amplify both our soul's hunger for meaning and all of the obstacles we create on our path of consciousness evolution.

An electronic web now surrounds our planet. Our ideas travel instantaneously to all points of the globe on electromagnetic waves and pulses of light. In the last decade, communications networks have advanced from wires to fiber optics, from interconnected radio and television grids to a world of billions of wirelessly communicating sensory devices, each with its own address in cyberspace. These collective systems for sharing thought have become the foundation of a new realm—the "Infosphere." Emerging from what French philosopher-priest Pierre Teilhard de Chardin called the shared "noosphere" of collective human thought, invention, and spiritual seeking, the Infosphere is now a field that engulfs our physical, mental, and etheric bodies and affects our dreaming and our cultural life.[1] In the mid-1960s, media sage Marshall McLuhan wrote that our nervous systems have been "extended" (via the "electric technologies" of sound and sight) beyond our physical bodies, drawing us all into a "global embrace":[2]

> Whereas all previous technologies (save speech itself) had, in effect, extended parts of our bodies, electricity may be said to have outered the central nervous system itself, including the brain.... The simultaneity of electric communication, also characteristic of our nervous system, makes each of us present and accessible to every other person in the world.[3]

Each new technology, he claimed, amplifies and extends the reach of different sense organs, changing our perceptions of our selves and of the world.

Think of how much information, in the form of radio energy, there is flying through the air, all around us, all over the world, right now and all the time. AM, FM, UHF, VHF, shortwave radio, television, CB radio, walkie-talkies, cellphones, cordless phones, telephone satellites, microwave relays, faxes, pagers, taxi calls, police, sheriff, hospitals, fire departments, telemetry, navigation, radar, the military, government, financial, legal, medical, the media, etc., etc., etc. Trillions and trillions and trillions and trillions of separate little bits of electronic information flying around the world through the air at all times. Think of that. Think of how busy the air is. Now realize this: A hundred years ago there was none. Nothing. Silence.

—George Carlin, *Brain Droppings*[4]

With each new sensory extension have come bursts of idealism and creativity as well as clouds of despair. The introduction of new technology has always been associated with profound changes in our views of reality and in global consciousness.[5] Socrates was unhappy about the transition from face-to-face speech to writing, and ever since the advent of the telegraph, modern critics have complained about the dangers of too-rapid telecommunications. As Erik Davis has pointed out in *TechGnosis*, we imbue each new communications technology with our highest spiritual aspirations and our deepest fears.[6] Electrical communication, with its ability to instantaneously move human intelligence beyond the confines of the physical body, has been the focus both of utopian dreams of deep social and spiritual connection and of profound terrors of "spiritual disassociation."[7]

Today, many see the global Internet as the beginnings of a true "global brain": a virtual community where people of different cultures find a worldcentric common language and develop new mental abilities and spiritual energies. To others, our communications technologies seem to hold only the basest elements of human nature. These critics claim that television and, more recently, video games and Web surfing have cut us off from each other, instilled false beliefs, and taught us to worship material goods. They point to teenagers with thumbs callused from sending text messages who cannot hold a face-to-face conversation. They see only gratuitous violence, demons, and dark ghosts inhabiting the virtual world of video games. They fear that wireless connectivity has forever breached the boundary between work and home, destroying what little rest we have eked out for the inner self. In the dire view of philosopher William Irwin Thompson, our bodies are cooking "in a global mulligan stew of electromagnetic noise," while according to one Buddhist scholar our minds are being "colonized" by the idea fragments—dubbed "memes" by Richard Dawkins—of commercial media.[8]

Yes, much of this critique may be true. As many "media ecologists" argue, our outer media have changed the balance of our senses and thus changed our lives, our culture, and our politics, maybe not as radically as techno-utopians and techno-naysayers have dreamed, but changed it nonetheless.[9] The electronic media amplify, distort, and attenuate our senses; change our awareness; and "mediate" our experiences. But we must also consider that these technologies are not just outside forces that appear out of nowhere to affect our consciousness and determine our future. They are also the products and the amplified reflections of our consciousness.

The relationship between consciousness and media works in both directions. In Howard Rheingold's words, "just as nature is not out there, beyond our skin, but the matrix from which consciousness emerges, technology is not out there, outside of what it means to be human."[10] All of our communications technologies—from the first telegraph signals traveling by wire to today's intelligent network routers, radio-frequency identification microchips, and global positioning satellites—have emerged from the creative collective mind. And that global mind is constantly growing and changing. In Jennifer Cobb's words, "we co-evolve with cyberspace as both we and it seek the next steps along the evolutionary path."[11]

Looking out into the Infosphere we find neither a dark, desolate, ghost-filled trap; nor a place of "cybergrace."[12] What we do see is a multilayered reflection of our own energetic communications systems in all of their emerging complexity, in all of their light and shadow. And behind these communications networks we find, as always, our equally multilayered and equally evolving communal consciousness. Our telecommunications engineers have brought forth electromagnetic and electro-optical devices of decreasing size, increasing complexity, increasing interactivity, and increasing self-awareness. I believe they have also given us a new way to describe the path of spiritual development that ancient esoteric teachings masked in arcane language, obscure references, and secret practices.[13] If the universe itself, as many philosophers tell us, is a field, not just of matter, but also of information, then the Infosphere must hold in its microcosm all of the levels of human experience, all our knowledge, all of our dramas of politics and power, and all of our dreams. This knowledge is encoded in our ubiquitous systems of telecommunications, and, yet, exactly because it is so omnipresent, to most of us it is still invisible.

This book is a guide to the layers of the Infosphere: It describes at each level of our outer technology a guiding metaphor that contains a wisdom lesson about the inner quality of human communications. Mapping the Infosphere will not replace mapping our souls. Yet in mapping it, we just might discover that we've been led away from chips and routers into the domain of the soul, finding in the technological structure and the social impacts of a specific telecommunications invention a guidepost for our own journey into greater consciousness. This is what I mean by "digital dharma": Seeing in everything—including the "teachings" of our web of electronic connectivity—an opportunity for conscious reflection on the deeper truth of our being.[14] Expanding "teleconsciousness" allows one to see what part of the energy body is engaged when one uses different communications forms. By turning our focus inward, this work suggests that a true healing of our cyber-addictions will come not from media reform protests or increased regulation, but from looking at our own shadow.

Every good map requires a legend, an organizing principle. For me, the evolution of the Infosphere appears to follow the "perennial wisdom" path—the universal truths and the values hierarchy that underlie all mystical religions. Integral philosopher Ken Wilber, in his elegant and groundbreaking book *The Spectrum of Consciousness*, describes this path as an overlapping (or nested) hierarchy of mental, moral/ethical, and spiritual development stages starting from the reptilian brain's focus on the self (safety, security and power), through the limbic system's more sociocentric outlook (with its attention to family, tribe, and community rules), to the neocortex's worldcentric view based on abstract ideals, to the transpersonal realms of the esoteric brain's spiritual connection to the Higher Self, Soul, or Godhead.[15] This evolutionary model forms the basis of contemporary Western consciousness studies, including the works of ecologist Duane Elgin, the aforementioned systems philosopher Ken Wilber, Creation theologian Matthew Fox, and transpersonal psychologists Carl Jung, Abraham Maslow, and Michael Murphy.[16]

I too, have followed the same road. I too, stop at the same development stages. However, as an energy healer I bring an additional reference frame to our exploration: the hierarchy of the body's seven esoteric communications centers. In the healing tradition from which my practice is drawn, a subtle energy field is believed to surround the human body. The transponders (transmitter-responders) that connect this field inward to the physical body and outward to the greater field of consciousness are the *chakras*

Figure 0.1. *Traditional chakra locations and symbols*

(Sanskrit for "wheels"). Each chakra aligns with a specific set of nerve clusters along the spinal column, each is associated with a different set of organs, and each has its own emotional-developmental resonance corresponding to the perennial wisdom.[17] A traditional depiction of the chakras is shown in figure 0.1.

Satprem, a disciple of the Indian sage Sri Aurobindo, writes that a chakra is "somewhat like a radio receiver tuned into particular wavelengths." He continues,

> [Each chakra] is linked with various planes of consciousness from which we constantly receive, most often unknowingly, all sorts of vibrations—subtle or physical, vital or mental, high or low—which account for our way of thinking, feeling and living, with the individual consciousness picking up certain vibrations rather than others, in accordance with its social background, traditions, education, etc.[18]

I have expanded on Satprem's description by directly associating each chakra with its corresponding communications theme and technology. Different media stimulate different energy centers, and, at the same time, as creations of human consciousness, they mirror the spiritual-emotional challenges associated with each center. By connecting the technologies of the Infosphere to their corresponding chakras, we discover that much of the debate over "media impacts" is really about the shadow side of our interior communications. We see in each of our external telecommunications networks not only a reflection of the state of our socio-cultural development, but also the core inner challenge each of us must overcome to move up the ladder of conscious communications. From this perspective, our media become our guides to advancement: our virtual ankle weights, barbells, and yoga stretches in our electronic ashram. One need not believe in the energy body and the chakras to follow the digital dharma path. Whatever system one follows—the mystical traditions mentioned above; the levels of ego, or *nafs*, of Sufi spiritual practice; the more down-to-earth "spiral dynamics" model developed by Clare Graves, Don Beck, and Christopher Cowan;

or even the "circuits of consciousness" theory of psychedelics pioneer Dr. Timothy Leary—the underlying spiral is the same.[19]

So please join me as we follow the chakras up the spine of the Infosphere and across cyberspace into greater complexity, and greater awareness. The first chapters focus on telegraphy and telephony: These communications technologies embody the foundation stage of our emotional-spiritual development, namely, our concerns for safety and connection. We then explore our relationships to others: our power to act, our feelings of love and compassion, and our ability to speak and discern the truth. We will see how these human issues are reflected back to us in our mass media of radio, television, and the Internet. Finally, we consider two transpersonal realms of consciousness. The first is the "eternal now" of the mystical third eye, our connection to intuition and powers of deep knowing; the second is the open, radiant crown, where we live fully connected to our spiritual selves as both creation and the Creator. The communications reflections of these higher levels of evolution are only now emerging: the "third eye" in the digital signal coding that makes possible high-definition television, video games, digital videodiscs (DVDs), and MP3 players; the "crown chakra" in the world of smart appliances, peer-to-peer networks, and the always-on intelligence of "pervasive computing." Table 0.1 points the way to the parallels that will be explored in depth in the following chapters.

It is my hope that having an expanded awareness of the lessons of the Infosphere—the work of our digital dharma—will speed up our individual and collective journey towards transformation. On the personal plane, by seeing how the light and shadow aspects of our emotional development issues play out in our use of communications media, we may find new goals for creating "clean" connections with those around us. As creators of our global network, we can practice an expanded "media ecology," understanding the "cultural memes" that are in play at each level of the Infosphere. We can insist that each technology be put to its highest use, remaining conscious of the "default application" that, without our vigilance, each media form will be enlisted to serve. Finally, as spiritual beings, we already know that the work is not about "fixing the Infosphere,"

Table 0.1. *Chakra functions and telecommunications parallels*

Dharma Level, Chakra Location, & Inner Work			Communications Technology and Related Dharma		
	1 Root	Security, "being safe," food/money, a connection to the earth		Radio-telegraphy, signal beacons, binary coding, radio-frequency identification, short message service	"Being Here," good ground connection
	2 Pelvis	Relationships, "I and Thou," the inner child, emotional memory and shadow		Telephony, analog waves, resonance, cell phones	Untangling cords of connection, intimacy calling, inner voicemail
	3 Solar Plexus	Personal power, autonomy, responsibility, shame issues		Broadcast Radio, one-to-many communications, podcasting	Sending a clear signal of self, who is the master's voice?
	4 Heart	Compassion, connection, love; also emotional addictions, grief		Television, the electronic hearth, interlaced scanning	Seeing the Other as oneself, stuffing the broken heart
	5 Throat	Communications, finding one's voice, listening with discernment		Peer-to-peer networks, connections across the grid	Filtering truth from lies, honesty and self-protection
	6 Third Eye	Deep seeing, going beyond the veil, revealing the codes of life		Digital compression, high-definition TV, MP3, virtual reality, signal coding, spread-spectrum	Breaking free from habitual decoding, living in the matrix
	7 Crown	Divine connection to Source; tapping the cosmic memory bank		Pervasive computing, Wi-Fi, global positioning satellites, Grid intelligence	Full-spectrum living, downloading from abundance

9

but about changing ourselves. Full "teleconsciousness" is just another tool to find in our outside world the lessons—the dharma—of inner transformation. Going on the Internet or playing a simulation game does not bring enlightenment, but these technologies do provide a new way of looking at our place in the fabric of being. In each interaction with the Infosphere, we have a choice whether to embrace the big picture and take in the full spectrum of data or to follow the path of limited input, and thus limited possibility.

For those open to exploring all aspects of the yoga metaphor, each chapter ends with a set of suggested exercises that use the metaphors of the Infosphere to "retune" our interior communications transponders. These exercises can be effective whether we envision chakras as whirling energy orbs or simply as symbols that remind us to be fully present to ourselves and to others at every level of our being. It is my intention in offering these exercises that as we open and heal these internal channels, not only will our personal communications become more whole and our spiritual flow more open, but also the Infosphere we have created to surround us will also mature and manifest its true spiritual potential.

FIRST-LEVEL
DIGITAL DHARMA

THE TELEGRAPH
OF ALIVENESS

First-level digital dharma is about mastering how we send out and respond to rudimentary signals of aliveness that encode the most basic message: "I am here. Is anyone else out there?"

At the first (or "base") level of human psychosocial development, the personality operates primarily in the biological and reflexive domain. Survival is the simple goal. Social organization boils down to "me versus everyone else." Because relationships are evaluated primarily on safety concerns, as the emerging personality struggles to distinguish itself as an individual, one's inner work involves discovering the "I"—and feeling strong enough to present it to the world.[1]

In the Infosphere, this core "Here I Am" message is built on binary signaling technologies, from the on-off pulses of the first electrical telegraph to the digital bits that now encode text messaging and radio-frequency identification and power all of cyberspace. The energetic calling out of one's existence starts at the subatomic level, where an electron, dropping from one quantum stage to the next, releases a single, discrete photon. This act of "calling out"—emitting a photon—"collapses" the photon's myriad of concurrent potential wave-function states into one physical object aligned with the expectations of the observer. As a quantum energy packet, the photon moves out of the realm of pure energy to become a wave/particle combination with one of many potential locations. There is no middle state in this quantum dance. An electron is at one level or another; there is no in-between. It is a zero or a one, resting or active, dead or alive, depending on how it is observed.[2]

At the cellular level, this same model applies. As long as we are alive, our cells constantly send out tiny energetic "I am here; is anyone else out there?" chemical, electrical, and audio coordination queries. The "music" of all of these microscopic instruments, writes systems theorist Ervin Laszlo, is one great jazz band, whose improvisation "ranges over more than seventy octaves":

> It is made up of the vibration of localized chemical bonds, the turning of molecular wheels, the beating of micro-cilia, the propagation of fluxes of electrons and protons, the flowing of metabolites and ionic currents within and among cells through ten orders of spatial magnitude.[3]

And these same queries are at the heart of first-level communications dharma, reflecting the personality's earliest work of differentiation, the work of moving from potential to specificity, from being part of the background to claiming one's individuality.

In the chakra model of energy yoga, these primitive messages are said to originate from the "root" transmitter at the base of the spine. The spiritual work of this center is to connect physical matter and the primal self. It channels the energy of the physical plane up through the feet to our "higher" centers, while at the same time connecting these centers back to the body. Its focus is on the individual's or clan's physical survival needs. The focus of much of its communication is on material exchange—labor and food.[4] Creation theologian Matthew Fox tells us that "solidarity is what the first chakra is all about: being solidly connected to the solid earth and the earth's home, which is the universe, and being in solidarity with all the sounds of the universe and its yearnings for life."[5] When one is fully present to the joyous side of first-level awareness, one takes in the pleasures of life. One sends out the existential declaration "*Hineini*"—Biblical Hebrew for "I am here"—meaning fully present, ready to be seen, ready to experience all of the joy and all of the fear of fully being in the physical world (figure 1.1). When this communications center is psychologically blocked, fears are sublimated. One's energy seems scattered, unfocused; boundaries are undefined and not respected. One looks for security in external things—money, power, and possessions—yet has a hard time receiving them. Everything becomes a struggle.[6]

Figure 1.1. Hineini: I Am Here

We can see many of these *Hineini* developmental issues reflected in the history of our "on-off" digital signaling technologies, starting with the first technology to extend our nervous system into the electrical domain—the telegraph. Its dots and dashes represented the first transmission of thought itself across "lines of lightning," as the electrical energy from one "station" pulsed across the wires to the electromagnetic coils of the receiving "sounder" miles away (see figure 1.2 on page 17).

The Riddle of Hebrew School

During my eighth and last year [of Hebrew School], just as I was relieved that my studies were going to end soon, I got tricked into being intrigued. Private sessions were scheduled with Rabbi Krinsky, who encouraged philosophic questions. So I seriously, if impudently, asked, "Why did I have to study Hebrew all this time, when all I've really learned is to hate Hebrew?" And he explained, "Judaism is a religion of doubt, not belief. The way to give thanks for intelligence is to use it to doubt the very things you've been told to accept. Realizing Hebrew School isn't about Hebrew is a sign you no longer need to go. It's not important for you to speak Hebrew. All the Hebrew anyone ever needs was taught the first day."

"What?" Madder than Dorothy must have been when she found out the transit truth of those ruby slippers in *The Wizard of Oz*, I balked, "Whaddaya mean? '*Shalom*,' and I was done?"

Rabbi Krinsky continued, "No, not *Shalom*. Not even the *She'mah*. But *Hee Nay Nee*—Here I am. Responding to your name when called during attendance. That's what really matters. The most important duty you have is to be present whenever you are called upon, whenever you are needed, whenever you can help. The point is to never be afraid to claim your right to be here, to stand up for yourself, and say '*Hee Nay Nee*. Here I am.'"

Okay, very tidy. But solving the riddle doesn't necessarily solve the problem. So the difficult part remains: That this most basic Hebrew "*Hee Nay Nee*" will take me not just one lesson, not just eight years, but a lifetime to learn to speak fluently.

—Flash Rosenberg, performance artist and filmmaker[7]

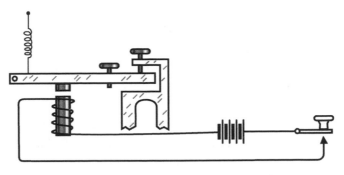

Figure 1.2. *Telegraph key and sounder*

Despite the utopian dreams of global intelligence with which techno-utopians of its day greeted the first transatlantic cable—they trumpeted it as an "instantaneous highway of thought" that would tie together the earth with "electric current, palpitating with human thoughts and emotions"[8]—the telegraph system was initially focused on first-level external concerns: the spheres of commerce; colonialism and war; and community prosperity and personal safety. By the end of the nineteenth century, the world was spanned

"Then there is electricity—the demon, the angel, the mighty physical power, the all-pervading intelligence!" exclaimed Clifford. "Is that a humbug, too? Is it a fact—or have I dreamt it—that, by means of electricity, the world of matter has become a great nerve, vibrating thousands of miles in a breathless point of time?"

"If you mean the telegraph," said the old gentleman ... "it is an excellent thing, that is, of course, if the speculators in cotton and politics don't get possession of it. A great thing, indeed, sir, particularly as regards the detection of bank-robbers and murderers."

—Nathaniel Hawthorne, *The House of the Seven Gables*[9]

by a network of almost a million miles of wires and almost one hundred thousand miles of undersea cable, a network amounting to what Tom Standage has called "the Victorian Internet."[10] Electrical messages delivered military orders, government and public safety alerts, weather warnings, and "buy and sell" directives across the world.

The telegraph network also brought a new sense of collective unease. People's sense of time and distance collapsed as cities were linked to cities and nations to nations, as giant spools of cable were unwound across the ocean floor. On some level people sensed that technology was about to push them all energetically closer. They understood that their sense of separateness was about to be challenged in a fundamental way: Communication could now take place without transportation, without embodiment—in a "contact achieved by the sharing of spiritual (electrical) fluids," as media scholar John Durham Peters so vividly puts it.[11] As media sage Marshall McLuhan observed, "In the same year, 1844, then, that men were playing chess and lotteries on the first American telegraph, Søren Kierkegaard published the *Concept of Dread*. The Age of Anxiety had begun."[12]

First-level concerns with physical safety, commercial market intelligence, the security of possessions, and fears of estrangement, along with high hopes for "universal communications," were all carried over from the dot-dash world of telegraphy into the new technology of "wireless."[13] Suddenly, new connections were now possible between people, countries, and (to some) the spirit world. In fact, much of the original vocabulary of communications over distance and time (such as transmitter, receiver, induction, channel, and resonance) was shared between the practitioners of esoteric spirituality and the early wireless pioneers. One of the earliest Spiritualist newspapers was called *The Spiritual Telegraph*, and one of the first attempts to market wireless stocks focused on convincing Christian Scientists (whose founder, Mary Baker Eddy, had written, "Spirit needs no wires or electricity to carry messages") that they would speed up the return of Christ by investing in this magic technology.[14]

At first generated by the discharge of stored electrical energy into giant spark gaps, then by the continuous-wave oscillation created by a tuned vacuum-tube circuit, radio waves crisscrossed the nascent Infosphere. "Wireless" was quickly adopted as a critical link to ships at sea: Powerful on-off pulses were adopted for use by radio navigation beacons and for ship-to-shore emergency signaling. The first documented "CQD" distress call was sent by wireless in 1899, and in 1909 a highly publicized sea rescue off the coast of Nantucket made "the marvels of wireless telegraphy" front-page news for days afterwards.[15] The technology was so critical to shipping that the nation's first radio broadcasting stations went silent for ten minutes every hour so that shore stations (figure 1.3) could listen for marine distress signals.

Figure 1.3. *U.S. Navy Wireless Station, Arlington, Virginia (1916)*

The famous "SOS" distress call, developed for its brevity when sent by Morse code, became forever associated with disasters at sea. The new distress call was pressed into service even before its official adoption in June 1912: In the Titanic disaster in April of that year, "SOS" was used and heard by wireless operators both at sea and at listening posts along the Atlantic seaboard. At a Marconi Wireless Company monitoring station on Long Island, one of the young men passing on the ship-to-ship emergency signals during the crisis was David Sarnoff, the future founder of RCA.[16]

While Sarnoff went on to build a commercial entertainment industry based on broadcasting (a third-level technology, as we shall see), a first-level electrical visionary of the early twentieth century took a different path. This visionary was the Serbian-American scientist Nikola Tesla, known for his invention of alternating-current generators, which at low frequencies made transporting electric power over great distances affordable and at high frequencies made the first continuous-wave wireless transmitters possible. Tesla believed that the earth itself was a huge power generator whose field could be tapped for free universal electricity. His vision was one of radiant energy cascading upwards from the earth's core, a projection into physical reality of what tantra yoga calls *kundalini*, the powerful force that lies dormant in the root chakra until awakened by deep spiritual practices.[17]

In a 1904 article entitled "World Telegraphy," Tesla also envisioned the expansion of radiotelegraphy into a universal text-messaging service, with transmission centers at all the world's major cities:

> A cheap and simple device, which might be carried in one's pocket may then be set up anywhere on sea or land, and it will record the world's news or such special messages as may be intended for it. Thus the entire earth will be converted into a huge brain, capable of response in every one of its parts.[18]

Tesla's dream is visible today in the millions of individual "text receivers" we carry strapped to belts or tucked in purses: our pagers, cellphones, GPS (global positioning satellite) trackers, and PDAs (personal digital assistants). These technologies, while also first used for business and finance, were quickly adapted to express the first chakra's beacon call of personal aliveness.

Today that beacon call has a singularly appropriate new mode of expression: short message service (SMS) technology, better known as text messaging or "texting." PDAs, cellphone-based text messaging, and Internet-based instant messaging or "IM," its linguistic and sociological close cousin, foster the exchange of mini-telegrams: notes in an abbreviated question-and-answer format too short for details (but not too short for flirting, for a Muslim divorce, or, for some Catholics in the Philippines, attending confession and receiving absolution).[19] Just as SMS telegraphs a phone call, IM telegraphs an e-mail. Quick and informal, instant messaging works in real time, demanding an immediate response. It has no time or space for deeper, more penetrating queries, or even for the simple hellos and goodbyes of telephone talk. In Maureen Dowd's words, "It's as if your id had a typewriter."[20]

In the business world, always-on telegram formats could lead to an oppressive, overcontrolled work environment that co-opts every waking moment in every location in the name of "more productive" work. But SMS is also being used to challenge the status quo. As Howard Rheingold has documented in *Smart Mobs*, it is already changing the social lives of teens and has made possible coordinated real-time group political action.[21] Smart message service was initially designed as an ancillary paging method for European cellphones. Because its messages are limited to 160 characters, developers assumed SMS would be primarily a business tool—for appointment reminders, stock quotes, and terse communiqués from the boss, for example. Yet within a decade of its introduction in 1991, tens of billions of SMS messages were being exchanged each month, primarily by young people in Europe and Asia,[22] and SMS was on its way to the United States. In the first quarter of 2004, 2.6 billion text messages were sent on cellphones in the United States, with more than seventy-five percent of teens using their phones for texting and games.[23] By the first quarter of 2005, this number had tripled, with total revenues from nonvoice services for the four largest U.S. mobile operators reaching $1.2 billion; a year later, these earnings had tripled.[24]

"Texting" is a perfect medium of adolescence, that time when kids start to push away and declare their individuality. Teens now spend hours using text to announce and reinforce their "being-ness" to their peers: sending out their location, testing their boundaries, calling attention to their cleverness, and coordinating their activities. In Tokyo they're called *oyayubisoko*, "the thumb tribe," who silently communicate without even looking at the key-pad. In Finland, the world leader in both Internet connections and cellphones per capita, texting is called *tekstata*; there it has become the tool of a generation that coordinates its entire social life through SMS. Whether sent by cellphone or pager, SMS is short, cheap, safely discreet, and, if preferred, anonymous. Mes-sages can be banal—little more than a casual "howz it goin'"—and still create the illusion of connection, giving an electronic nod that keeps the community connected at the most basic acknowledg-ment level.[25]

Other messages can be more direct. One Australian cellphone company is now hosting "love-in" events for its subscribers. Attendees (wearing large name badges with their text addresses) are encouraged to send SMS pickup lines to each other. The raunchier messages are displayed on a large public screen, as are the replies. And, in the United States, if you need help with your pickup lines, Comedy Central will provide your cellphone text display with a new one every day (for $2.99 per month). Of course, as Tom Foley discovered at the end of 2006, sending traceable SMS pick-ups is not such a good idea if one is a U.S. Congressman and the recipient is an underage page![26] As an extension of adolescent power, IM and SMS have sadly also become tools of teenage social cruelty. The ease of instant messag-ing—when combined with a typical adolescent's lack of (first-level) boundary control, budding sense of (third-level) personal power, and underdeveloped (fourth-level) empathy skills—has led to a spate of electronic taunting and bullying in America's middle and high schools.[27]

In addition to its social parallels to adolescence, SMS messaging mimics the evolution of biological transmissions, in which individual cellular-level calls stimulate more sophisticated "coordination broadcasts" and a kind of organic cohesion. Internally, every living cell is constantly sending and receiving a "cacophony of messages from all around the body: instructions, queries, corrections, requests for assistance, updates, notices to divide or expire." Each cell sings out its aliveness in weak pulses of light at specific wavelengths and intervals.[28] Medical researchers fighting infection are finding, not the random acts of solitary bacteria, but an information-based colony with specialized tasks, coordinated by protein-based, "quorum sensing" data broadcasts. Howard Bloom expands on this metaphor as follows:

> Modern research hints that primordial communities of bacteria were elaborately interwoven by communications links. Their signaling devices would have been many: chemical outpourings with which one group transmitted its findings to all in its vicinity, fragments of genetic material drifting from one end to the other of the community, and a variety of other devices for long distance data broadcasting.[29]

A unique new social phenomenon springing from texting is the "flash mob": the spontaneous convening—and rapid dispersal—of short-lived temporary action communities. Some gather for fun, like the group called to "gather at the washing machine display in a department store in the city of Dortmund, Germany, eat a banana, and leave."[30] Others have more serious goals. In the political arena, organizers can text potential voters to coordinate protests and election rallies. In many countries with restricted press, SMS and instant messaging have become the preferred tools of mass "e-mobilization."

If television helped bring down the Berlin Wall and the fax machine helped protesters organize during the Tiananmen Square protests, cellphone text messaging, also known as SMS (short message services), may be the new political tool for activists. In tech-savvy nations like South Korea, but more so in controlled societies like China and the Middle East, text messaging has been fomenting what some experts call a "mobile democracy." Because it is unmonitored and cheap, it provides an underground channel for succinct uncensored speech. Demonstrators use it to mobilize protests, dodge authorities, and fire off political spam. It has also enabled them to engineer collective action at unprecedented speed.

—Cathy Hong, *Christian Science Monitor*, June 30, 2005 [31]

According to Rheingold's analysis of this phenomenon, the first head of state to lose power to an SMS-coordinated "smart mob" was President Joseph Estrada of the Philippines. In Bolivia, text-message-directed protests are also credited with the resignation of Gonzalo Sánchez de Lozada. When President George Bush traveled to England in November 2003, he was tracked by protesters who sent his location by SMS to subscribers across the country. And protesters in New Zealand used SMS to coordinate marches against genetically modified food production in their country. [32]

In Venezuela, supporters of President Hugo Chávez were called to rally in his behalf by "a mixture of low-tech '*cacerolazos*' (pot-banging) and high-tech cellphones and pagers." According to local reporters, the United States, fearful of such SMS use, had a Navy warship stationed in waters just offshore attempt to jam cellphone signals and pagers in Venezuela during the coup. [33] The fall of the center-right government in Spain after the March 2004 terrorist attacks has been attributed to the lightning-like spread of the

"¡Pásalo (pass it on)!" call message on the country's cellphone screens. In the United States, "Flashmobs for Dean" was the subject of a series of *Doonesbury* cartoons, and an SMS-linked bicyclist circled the 2004 Republican Convention "spray-chalking" anti-Bush slogans sent to him via e-mail and text.[34]

The electrical mirroring of first-chakra signaling into the Infosphere will become nearly universal with the explosion of radio-frequency identification (RFID) technology. In a typical RFID system, each individual product is equipped with a tiny, inexpensive tag with its own electronic signature.[35] These products are similar in operation to the transponders used in drive-through tollbooths, where the device in the car responds to a query signal from the tollbooth with its unique code, triggering a charge against the user's account. As this technology gets cheaper and smaller, it is likely that our physical environment will be flooded with millions of these "calling out" radio transmissions. Tiny, silently signaling tags—often as small as a grain of sand—are already riding in bulk shipping containers, wholesale pharmaceutical cartons, and warehouse inventories; soon they will be in airline baggage tags and also in consumer packaging, where they will prevent fraud, track deliveries, and provide accurate, near-real-time inventory control.[36] Some schools are experimenting with student RFID necklaces for security and attendance tracking (with mixed initial responses), and RFID bracelets are available for rent at an increasing number of large amusement parks.[37] The technology is helping nursing homes automatically track elderly residents who also have a "help alert" button on their badge.[38] Our currency too may someday have embedded signaling to track money laundering and foil counterfeiting.[39]

Adding a GPS receiver chip[40] to an RFID transmitter will allow any object, person, or animal to broadcast its location as well as its identity. Such GPS-RFID tags will help soldiers locate friend or foe even in the dark of night. Pet owners will be able to set the boundaries for their pets' travels: A radio GPS receiver on the pet's collar will constantly track the animal's position, and when it crosses outside the set safety area, the collar will send a message to a tracking service, which will in turn send the owner an e-mail or SMS text message with a map of the animal's exact location.[41] These same features are coming to our cellphones as well. A federal mandate required that, by the end of 2005, all cellphones display their location during a 911 call. As a result, all the U.S. carriers put GPS chips in their cellphones. Soon our cellphones will tell us with digital precision, "You are here." For anxious parents (just as for pet owners), these phones can send a text message saying, "Your child has just left school." For the parents of teenagers, such a phone can tell not only where its owner is, but also whether the child is in a vehicle and how fast it is traveling.[42] That is, assuming the phone remains with its owner!

Location sensitive radio-frequency identification is beginning to support a (second-level) "relationship-making" component. Communicating lapel screens give business conference attendees a start on conversation. The devices feature an LCD display that communicates with other badges in close proximity, recognizing and broadcasting greetings specifically for the fellow badge-holder.[43] A number of online dating services are offering a "proximity dating" option that allows people to rate on a five-point scale what they are looking for in a partner. When someone having the right profile comes within range, the compatible individuals' phones will buzz and the profiles will be shared via SMS.[44] Our world is fast approaching the time when every moving object could be assigned its own RFID transmitter. On one level, this world could look like the ultimate paranoid security state, where every object and person is tagged with its own code number, where large corporations and "homeland security" organizations can track our every move—making RFID a true "mark of the Beast" for those who await the Apocalypse.[45] Indeed, in giving core first-chakra tools to immature beings, our technology has magnified the power of those who want to "keep us in our place," and it has also empowered those who want to know where we are so they can badger us to buy their stuff. But like any tool, our first-level media also present us with wisdom opportunities: They suggest that we use our signaling technologies to practice a yoga of deep listening.

The first chakra "grounds" us on the earth, our common home. Networked grids of sensors will soon cover the earth, extending our collective electronic nervous system to new realms. What if we insisted that we use this new awareness to reveal the planet's physical health: to electronically track and share the conditions of the planet's crust; the condition of its forests, lakes, and streams; the encroachment of the deserts; the thinning of the ozone layer; the decline of the ocean's diversity? What if society used these signaling technologies to monitor and display in real time not just our personal wealth, but also our energy consumption or the number of malnourished children in the world? The technology is available. The choice is ours.[46]

Can our first-chakra technologies remind us to recognize each person, animal, organism, or living cell as a living transmitter of spiritual energy? What if our sea of "messaging" devices is a physical embodiment of the truth that every object in the universe is calling to us with its own unique song, that consciousness extends all the way down to the most elemental level, that every living object wants to radiate its aliveness to the world, that the universe itself (as string theory indicates) is the sum of all these vibrations? Our choice is to take these lessons inside, living our dharma fully present, "walking the walk," grounded at every step along life's path, sure of our own identity, comfortable honoring the identity of others.[47]

LIVING IN FULL FIRST-LEVEL TELECONSCIOUSNESS

The developmental work associated with the first chakra is that of building appropriate boundaries, experiencing life fully, and, when it is time, dissolving these walls and leaving the physical body.[48] Healthy first-level consciousness feels safe, drawing to it the security of food, shelter, clothing, and money. These prerequisites enable one to experience life fully in the body, without rushing to seek refuge in mental abstraction or "higher" spiritual realms. When this energy center is compromised by poor physical, mental, or spiritual health or by trauma or fear, we don't feel "grounded." We lose our sense of place. We no longer know where we belong or where it is safe to play. Our survival needs get displaced into unhealthy behaviors such as binge eating or shopping, or to the other lower chakras involved in sexuality or power, thereby distorting the relationship to others and to oneself.

The same is true in the domain of telecommunications: Without a reference ground, there is no way to decode binary information, to distinguish a one from a zero. All that remains is noise. Without a connection to the earth and to the physical body, all signals become mere static. In the domain of personal teleconsciousness, one's *Hineini* beacon starts drifting from its assigned frequency, and all other first-chakra communications cease, replaced by an automatic repetition of the *dot-dot-dot, dash-dash-dash, dot-dot-dot* SOS cry.

Looking around us, we can see how the overuse of first-chakra technologies reflects this loss of earth connection: The binary telegraph inundated the public with stock market readings and "futures" prices that carried no sense of the people and places displaced by global economic forces. Always-available Internet connections, portable PDAs, and walkie-talkie cellphones can seduce us into staying "on duty." RFID transmitters, like the jangling body jewelry and skin piercing on rebellious youth, insist repeatedly, "Notice me now." These same devices, when used surreptitiously, can tell Big Brother our every step. This is an overcontrolled world of no zero state, no rest!

Even though we live in midst of here-and-now, fear-based applications of first-level technologies, I believe that these technologies have something deeper to tell us about our dharma. Could not every SMS call, every transmitting RFID tag, be a concrete metaphor reminding us to be accessible to others, to see and be seen, to hear and fully respond to the other?[49] Acknowledging each active node on a network and "polling" its readiness to send a message is the basis of digital packet communications.[50] Likewise, recognizing, and then honoring, each other's calls of aliveness is the first lesson of our digital dharma.

The root chakra constantly transmits and receives invisible pulses of aliveness: "I am here . . . Who's there?" Some part of our awareness is always checking out these energetic broadcasts that surround us. We subconsciously sense the needs and fears as well as the strength of others—and they are busy registering our transmissions as well. What message are we sending out to the world? Are our broadcasts welcoming or threatening? Are we securely grounded? Can we tap the energy pulses from our earth connection below us? Can we hold the love we receive, or does it leak out the bottom of our "inner container"?

The challenge of first-level digital dharma is to acknowledge the calling-out signals of our neighbors. Before saying anything, can you "take in" the other being? I have tried to make it a practice to stop at least two or three times each day for a moment to observe my personal cellular pulses: my breath, the blood in my veins, the thoughts generated by my always-chattering busy mind. My meditation practice also takes me back to this state of neutral observation. In silence, I visualize extending my first chakra into the earth, acknowledging the physical world in which we all live. From this safe stillness, I then visualize peace flowing into my body and see my being emerging from pure potential. I ask to recognize the beingness of others, celebrating the universal pulse of human aliveness. I join that chorus with a profound *Hineini*, sending a joyous "I Am" signal to all those around me.

FIRST-LEVEL TELECONSCIOUSNESS VISUALIZATION

Tuning in to Existence

In a seated position, with your feet on the floor, imagine extending the energy cloud of your root chakra to the ground. Picture the excess electrical charge in this chakra seeking to ground with the core of the earth. Allow yourself to merge into the solidity of the earth. Expand this connection. Quiet your mind. Feel cords of energy extending down, not only from your base but also from your feet, into the center of the earth. Feel the earth's warmth rising up into your body. Charge your field with this magnetic energy from the dynamo that resides in the center of the planet's molten core. Feel the pulses within your own body: the "lub-dub" beating of your heart, the blood in your veins, the rise and fall of your chest with each breath. Go deeper into these rhythms. Can you hear the circulation in your ears? The tingle of the nerves in your skin? The electricity in your spine?

Slowly lie down. Visualize each body part coming into Being, infused with energy. Rest. Connect with your first chakra. See it pulsing your own special radio "call sign" for all to hear. Grounded and secure in being alive, allow your first chakra to be an energetic lighthouse that announces, "I am here!" Know where you are, strengthen that signal, and let it radiate out to the universe. Open the space; know that you deserve to feel this energetic connection.

Now bring into your awareness someone who needs acknowledgment (perhaps a friend, co-worker, or family member). Tune to his or her first-chakra "broadcast." Picture yourself sending an acknowledgment signal without judgment or any content other than "message received; I know where you are." In the same way, send an acknowledgment out to all the nodes in your network (friends, lovers, enemies, political leaders). And send one also within, gently, to any dark places that need illumination.

Next, move out to the Infosphere, seeing all living beings as a chorus of "I Am" transmitters—from the simplest virus to each and every human. See the planets, the supernovas and pulsars in far-off galaxies, all radiating their own unique beacons. Stay in this place for as long as you like.

Finally bring your attention gently back to your own first-level signal generator. Let it join this universal chorus. Once it is clear and strong, bring your awareness back to your body, to your breath, to your own pulsing aliveness. Wiggle your toes. Gently open your eyes. Return to waking consciousness, but continue to sense your underlying connection to all life.

SECOND-LEVEL
DIGITAL DHARMA

REACH OUT
AND TOUCH SOMEONE

Second-chakra communications work shifts from a preoccupation with "I statements" to managing emotional exchange with others around us: that is, learning how to appropriately honor our desire to connect with the "Thou." One advances beyond "yes/no" declarations, moving from quantum-as-particle to quantum-as-wave, from the solidity of the earth to the realm of the oceans. One learns the dance of amplitude, frequency, resonance, harmonics; the dance of pain and pleasure and give and take that is relationship—all flowing symbolically from the second chakra.

The second chakra is the transponder of attraction and the center of one's creativity. From here, one radiates the primordial drive for union embedded in our very protons and electrons. It is from here that we seek on the physical plane to "reach out and touch someone."[1] In the spiritual domain, this energy at its simplest level fuels the hunger to connect with (and keep happy) powerful nature spirits[2] and at a more "sophisticated" level, the desire to merge with one's vision of the Divine Beloved.[3]

When open and free, this chakra radiates the dancing pleasure of connection—to the inner self as well as to others. When repressed or blocked, second-level energy often becomes polarized, drawing to it all the people and all the emotional situations that one tries so hard to avoid. Energy healer Ambika Wauters tells us that a closed second chakra can also reflect a martyr complex, the pattern of life where fulfillment is always postponed. When stressed, this connection-craving center calls out to anyone. Obsessive talking and poor relationship boundaries are signs of unbalanced second-level energy. At its most extreme, the second chakra's "shadow side" engenders seduction and unhealthy emotional entanglements and also holds the resulting energy of shame.[4]

All of these qualities we bring to the most personal and intimate Infosphere technology: the telephone. Marshall McLuhan understood this technology's link to deepest emotion when he asked:

> Why should the phone create an intensive feeling of loneliness? Why should we feel compelled to answer a ringing public phone when we know the call cannot concern us? Why does a phone ringing on stage create instant tension?... The answer to all of these questions is simply that the phone is a participant form that demands a partner, with all the intensity of electric polarity.[5]

A ringing telephone demands our attention not only with its sweet siren ring, but also with its promise of a live person on the other end.

Indeed, a quality of intense longing has permeated the social history of telephony from the moment of its birth. In 1876, the first words heard through a working telephone were "Mr. Watson, come here, I want to see you!"—Alexander Graham Bell's famous cry for help after he spilled battery acid on himself, an utterance wholly unlike the declarative "What hath God wrought" clicked out by Samuel F. B. Morse to announce the birth of the telegraph.[6] Bell's urgent plea (on a device he intended for the transmission of musical tones to the deaf) really heralded the coming technology of feelings, of want and desire. Erik Davis tells us it signaled the creation of "the ultimate animist technology . . . an inert thing full of voices."[7]

> Today I have seen that which yesterday I should have deemed impossible. Soon lovers will whisper their secrets over an electric wire.
>
> —Sir William Thomson, later Lord Kelvin, upon testing Bell's earliest telephone set at the 1876 Centennial Exhibition in Philadelphia.[8]

Shared talk is an intimate act, and the telephone—which makes people seem like they're in your head—invokes this proximity with every call. The shaman-like "whisper in the ear—the lips of the speaker literally at the ear of the listener [is] by and large the domain of lovers and loved ones," says media ecology scholar Paul Levinson, who continues: "And yet this is exactly the acoustical distance obtained in a phone conversation, whether the party at the other end is one's lover, an unknown voice offering a great deal on insurance, or a wrong number." Not knowing the identity of the "off-scene" voice at the other end of the wire is truly emotionally unnerving, "obscene."[9]

The call to social intimacy has always been part of the telephone connection experience. At first, like the telegraph, the telephone was put to "appropriate" first-level uses and was marketed exclusively to professionals, businessmen, and government officials. In fact, telephone "visiting" was frowned upon as trivial and feminine. Residential telephones appeared only in upper-income households, where servants were expected to answer them.[10] Eventually, however, domestic demand for this new convenience won out. By 1907, AT&T had stopped lecturing its customers on proper telephone etiquette and embraced the notion that every American deserved equal access to the system. Abandoning the argument that efficiency demanded centralized authority, the firm now declared: "Every Bell Telephone is the Center of the System."[11]

Slowly at first, then more rapidly as prices fell in the 1920s, the telephone extended its reach into the home. It moved from competing in the rational text-based domain of the telegraph (the male language of business, government, and the military) to the emotional-subjective (female) domain of the human voice; from the ordered, left-brain-dominant realm of the alphabet to the more flowing, conversational, metaphoric, and musical space of the right brain.[12] Telephone operators were no longer rowdy young male technicians but young women from good families (figure 2.1); a hard, male technology was softened by the feminine "voice of service with a smile."[13]

Figure 2.1. *Switchboard operators*

Coupling the force of electricity to the second chakra's hunger for connection stirred intense interpersonal emotions. The effect was explosive. Initially an instrument of control by the father and husband, the telephone became a tool of female liberation. In the cities, it created new jobs for women as operators and secretaries. In rural areas, the shared party line ended the farm wife's isolation forever.[14] In home after home, the phone subverted the locked front door, providing young people with connections to the world outside, right under the noses of stern parents. As early as 1900, stories began to appear in industry journals of telephone seductions and elopements and of scandalous young women flirting over the phone from bed, stories that in many ways predicted the advent of today's multi-million-dollar phone sex industry. As telephone historian Robert MacDougall writes, "lovers, criminals, and pranksters shaped the uses and meaning of the telephone as surely as did politicians and engineers." The early phone network was not just an extension of the telegraph, a tool of the business world, but also "a lawless thing, at times dangerous, at others sexualized, at others juvenile. It was used not only to bridge distances, but to breach customs and break rules."[15]

Talking on the phone invites second chakra emotional connection. Who hasn't spent hours whispering deep secrets to a best friend or lover? Of course, long-distance intimacy brings its own vulnerabilities, such as being secretly recorded or spilling out one's most personal thoughts after a few too many drinks![16] And beyond social lapses, the emotional charge of even everyday telephone talk can make us physiologically vulnerable. The brain's "on the phone" operational state is closer to dreaming than to its everyday, externally oriented mode. In a recent test, lab volunteers experienced a significant reduction in their ability to process visual stimuli while talking on cellphones. Other studies have reported that talking on a cellphone increased the risk of having an accident four-fold.[17]

This is the story of a CPA who was also a college instructor, Rick. He had gone to lunch at a local mall. Coming out of the mall there is an entrance to a local highway. Rick was talking to his banker on his cellphone. He stopped, looked right, looked left directly into the eyes of the school bus driver who was traveling the legal 55 mph . . . and then, while talking, drove directly into the path of the school bus. No more Rick.

—From a collection of cellphone accident stories on the Web site of the radio show *Car Talk*[18]

Today, more than one hundred years after Alexander Graham Bell made what was essentially the first "911" call, the second chakra's drive for authentic connection still underlies this technology. Lovers everywhere talk the night away; social networks of all kinds are supported by cellphone "linkups"; conference call "phone bridges" provide group therapy on the most intimate topics. Numerous support groups for those facing grief, addictions, and life-threatening diseases quietly thrive on phone conferencing systems provided by universities, hospitals, and social-service agencies. Somehow, at times of crisis, the anonymous intimacy of the telephone allows for deep connection, even among strangers. Telephone counseling has been shown to improve recovery rates for patients taking antidepressant drugs.[19] Even after exchanging long e-mails, most computer daters rely on the telephone to "energetically check out" their potential partners before agreeing to meet in person.

Net-based telephony now makes international talk so cheap that accepting calls from and hanging out with distant total strangers has become a new social phenomenon, though it has some precedent in the culture of ham radio. Some folks practice their foreign language skills by calling native speakers, while student radio interviewers at Swarthmore's "War News Radio" using Skype (a popular Internet phone service) had no problem making "cold calls" to homemakers, students, and business owners in war-ravaged Baghdad. Unlike instant messaging, which is essentially anonymous, Web-phone contact creates an immediate intimate "confessional connection" between newfound acquaintances: "With voice," one regular user told a *New York Times* interviewer, "you cannot hide from the other person." [20]

Of course, like every other communications technology, the telephone has spawned a brisk—if virtual—sex trade. Now a billion-dollar industry, "adult" phone services provide second-chakra stimulation on the go. [21] Erotic fantasies are charged by the minute. So lucrative is the phone-sex business that some of the poorest countries in the world are willingly cashing in. The fiscal strategies can be, well, creative. For example, remote micronations allow "adult services" to be rerouted through their networks in exchange for a percentage of the call charges, even though the calls neither originate nor connect within their borders. These calls are virtually routed to and billed as incoming long distance calls by countries such as Guyana and the Dutch Antilles. Niue, a tiny island protectorate of New Zealand, routes sex calls from Japan.

As early as 1901, the English radio engineer William Ayrton wrote of a time when everyone would have his or her own wireless system with its own "secret frequency":

> If a person wanted to call a friend he knew not where, he would call in a loud, electromagnetic voice, heard by him who had the electromagnetic ear, silent to him who had it not. "Where are you?" he would say. A small reply would come, "I am at the bottom of a coal mine, or crossing the Andes, or in the middle of the Pacific." Let them think of what that meant, of the calling which went on every day from room to room of a house, and then think of that calling extending from pole to pole. [22]

A decade later, Columbia University engineering professor Michael Pupin told the *New York Times* that such a device might not be such a good idea: "It's bad enough as it is, but with the wireless telephone one could be called up at the opera, in church, in our beds. Where could one be free from interruption?" [23]

Today's ceaseless traffic over ubiquitous cellphone channels certainly proves Ayrton's foresight. Phones in our cars, pockets, purses—and hooked in our ears—keep us connected, providing continual reassurance that we are not alone. Young children now routinely wear pagers for (first-level) security and have their own real, working cellphones preprogrammed to call home. And anyone confronting the babble of ringtones and overheard conversations can testify to the correctness of Pupin's reservations about the new technology![24] Cellphones free teens from parental eavesdropping but also make them more accessible and accountable. A recent attempt to enforce a ban on mobile phones in New York City public schools caused a near-rebellion from parents, who now consider the device an "urban umbilical cord" that holds families together and allows them to feel that their children are safe once they leave the house. On the other hand, some college administrators worry that cellphone connections to home are keeping entering freshmen students from integrating into their new campus community. Worse yet, "are the constant calls from their parents, many of whom are more nervous than their children."[25]

Phones are all about staying connected at the second-chakra level. In a front-page story in 2003, the *New York Times* described how the cellphone has become a cultural lifeline for the city's immigrant cabbies—from "Punjabi cousins" to Sherpas from Nepal and soccer-crazed Salvadorans—connecting them to families back home and "to the humor and commiseration of other drivers braving the same lonely streets."[26] In the despair of the Kosovo refugee camps (and more recently in New Orleans after the Hurricane Katrina disaster), lines outside the few satellite mobile phone tents were as long as those at the kitchens. A few numbers scribbled on a piece of paper—a country code, followed by a city code and seven numerals—was a valuable possession, a link to lost loved ones and relatives around the world.[27] In the most rural areas of African Congo, enterprising barefoot entrepreneurs catch distant cellphone signals in tree-house towers and sell the precious invisible access to families hungry for contact with loved ones working far from their home villages. In Bangladesh, more than 260,000 "phone ladies" have received microcredit loans to provide village phone service for the poor all over the country, earning the company's founder (and its bank) the 2006 Nobel Peace Prize. Peasant farmers in Senegal barter their crops via wireless connections, and in Ghana, some even choose to be buried in giant mobile phone coffins (figure 2.2).[28] In America, this need for phone visiting has become a reliable revenue source for budget-strapped jails that charge families of inmates up to seven times the regular cost of an outside collect call (which in turn, is many times the standard rate),[29] prompting a *New York Times* editorial to call it the "Bankrupt-Your-Family Calling Plan."[30]

To many, talking on the phone is virtually synonymous with love. Behavior over the phone also reflects the consequences of injury to the chakra center associated with this desire. A person with an

Figure 2.2. *Cell-phone coffin in Ghana*

overcompensating second chakra is often emotionally codependent, bouncing from the highs and lows on the waveform of emotional communications, needing to be connected at all times. Such people have a hard time recognizing boundaries, and if the first chakra has also been compromised, they are usually afraid of standing alone in their own psychological space. To some degree, we all need to know that we're not alone. Thus, it is not surprising to find every urban roof and rural hill topped with a cell tower and companies like Apple coming out with $600 "iPhones." Telecom moguls may have erected those towers for profit, but it is the universal human need for connection and validation from the other that makes the technology both inevitable and successful. As the late columnist Herbert Stein observed, "You may think you are checking on your portfolio, but deep down you are checking on your existence."[31]

For some, even fake conversation seems to be preferable to none: witness the phenomenon of "reaching out to no one," that is, pretending to be on the phone as a way of avoiding interacting with nearby "real" people who may want your attention.[32] Then for the truly confused, there's "Vivienne," a $6-per-month downloadable cellular girlfriend, complete with a fondness for movies and bars. She expects you to send her virtual presents, and, if you decide to marry her online, her (virtual) mother will call your cellphone at all hours, "to ask where you are and whether you've been treating her daughter right."[33]

Thus far, we've looked at how cellphones reflect and support second-level digital "relationship dharma." Cellphone communications technologies also reflect other developmental stages. Caller ID and ID "blocking"—determining who enters your private phone space—is a first-chakra issue. One's "tribal identity" (a third-level issue) can be strengthened by subscribing to a lifestyle package of video clips, news, and games customized for a niche demographic: sports fanatics, Disney kids, teenagers, hip-hop fans.[34] Purchasing (at prices up to $3 each) and broadcasting one's personal ringtone is a more public identity statement. Worldwide, tone creation and distribution has become a $3-billion industry. The business is so promising that music companies are creating in-house divisions to sell tones via download and from subway vending machines.[35] Later chapters will show how Net-connected camera phones also play out digital dharma challenges at the fourth, fifth, and sixth levels.

On a spiritual level, when we embrace second-level teleconsciousness, we become willing to try connections beyond the safety of habitual boundaries. We tap our inner creativity and our ability to make and appreciate art. We listen to the voice of our "magical child" and we pay attention to our dreams. We tune in fully to the heart-based stories of others. These qualities are not entirely absent in telephone-based technology and in fact inform some of its best applications. Many communities are developing cellphone-guided neighborhood tours and local living histories. The *New York Times* recently featured the story of an artist who has recruited his neighbors to record stories about the love life in their building; another uses stickers with text-messaging numbers to alert passers-by that something of interest is near. The BBC has recently placed small plaques containing barcodes along some of the country's scenic and historical walks, and hikers with specially equipped camera phones can scan the codes and receive interactive audio and video tours.[36] Internet-based, inexpensive telephone conferencing will connect us to our different communities of interest, worldwide. And we must not forget, that like any yoga practice, moderation and rest are part of the package—we must not forget to periodically mute the ringer and listen to the silence of Being.

LIVING IN FULL SECOND-LEVEL TELECONSCIOUSNESS

I visualize my second-chakra communications transponder as a soft orange cloud that spreads out in front and back of my pelvis, seeking contact with others. It is a true "analog" interface: Its energy rises and falls in rhythmic waves, in constant harmonic modulation with the waves surrounding it. This chakra, silently transmitting my deepest feelings and receiving those of others, is my link to my inner emotional body. This is also the transponder that "entrains" me with my loved ones (that is, puts me in synchronous resonance with them) by opening to their signals of love or fear, joy, or distress.[37]

In childhood the second-chakra center is attuned to one's immediate caregivers. In older children, communications extend to family and friends, and in young adults, to mates and mentors. A fully open and thriving second chakra brings healthy relationships, sensual pleasure, and playful creativity. Blocked second-chakra energy can lead to unhealthy, dependent relationships and doubts about one's ability to love. Unblocking here requires acknowledging—and if necessary transforming—one's emotional and energetic links to others. "Calling" someone—whether on the phone, emotionally, or psychically—requires that our "lines of connection" be open and free flowing.

The second chakra holds early lessons about relationships, as well as buried feelings and emotions. Healing means opening the body, releasing tension, and expanding one's capacity to experience love. With a clear emotional center, even a phone call can create intimacy and love. The work of "communications yoga" involves clearing old attachments and "disconnecting" from trapped conversations and outmoded belief systems.

The second chakra is the universal party line, connecting our innermost hopes and desires, linking us to the voicemail from the inner magical child. Healing the second chakra allows emotional flow, intimacy, and connection. It makes us ready to connect with the divine that is love, both lover and beloved.

SECOND-LEVEL TELECONSCIOUSNESS VISUALIZATIONS

Checking Your Inner Voicemail

Sit in a comfortable chair. Relax. . . . Take a deep breath and release all tension as you exhale. Let go of your thoughts, and gently float away from your physical body.

Know that it is safe. Feel yourself rising up to the ceiling
.... Gently pass through the roof, up into inviting soft
clouds. Rise higher and feel the sun. Ask your Higher Self
for second-chakra healing.

Continue to drift up and away, moving to your left.
Notice the clouds thinning out and a large green forest
coming into view below you. Set your intention to descend,
and feel yourself slowly drifting down to a small, protected
clearing in the woods. The ground is soft. A river is nearby. You feel the warm sun on your face. You see a path
back into the forest, and you know that this is the direction you must go. Follow the path until it leads you
down a flight of steps, each bringing you closer to your
second chakra.

After the last step you see a path, leading to a larger
clearing. You hurry to it, and find yourself at one end of
a meadow, looking up into the hills. A path lies ahead, and
you notice that someone is walking down it toward you.

It is a small person. It's you at an earlier age. Upon
meeting, you hug and hold each other. The child-you
takes your hand and leads you to a nearby stream. You
smell the flowers and feel the purifying mist. After walking a bit, you see the entrance to a cave.

The two of you go inside. There's a soft warm light.
You go deeper back into the cave . . .

On a table is a chest. You open it. Inside is an old
answering machine with two cassette tapes. One says
"incoming messages." You take out it out and hold it to
your ear. This is a magical place, so even without a player, you instinctively know what's on this tape: the messages from your creative inner child. Listen with love and
nonjudgment. Acknowledge his or her needs and dreams.
Acknowledge the injuries and wounds of the past.

Pick up the second tape. This is your inner message to other callers. Do you want to change it? Imagine a new greeting being recorded on this tape. Make this your new second-chakra approach to the world of relationships. Mentally hit "record" and send it out.

Now place the machine back in the chest. Retrace your steps. See your child-self smiling at the cave entrance. Hug once again; watch him or her skip off to play. Turn and will yourself back to the meadow. Take a few moments to enjoy the peace of this clearing in the forest. Now slowly come back to awareness. . . . Wiggle your toes and fingers and open your eyes.

Clearing the Cords

Sit in a comfortable chair. Relax. . . . Follow your breath to any place of tension. Release it. Let go of any thoughts. Allow yourself to float gently away from your physical body, moving your awareness out into the energy field that surrounds you. Ask your Higher Self to support you in this second-chakra clearing meditation. When you feel a confirmation signal, in your mind's eye bring before you an elevator. Its doors open and you step inside. You feel safe.

On the wall is a big button. It says "Second Chakra Communications Room." You press it and the doors close. You feel the elevator descending. When you are ready, it stops and the doors open onto a dimly lit hallway, down which you begin to walk. Passing unmarked locked doors, you turn a corner and see a doorway with warm light spilling out from around its frame. You know this is the entrance you are seeking.

The door is labeled "Second Chakra Communications Equipment." You open the door and step inside, and as you do the light seems to get brighter. There before you is an old-fashioned telephone switchboard with lots of tangled cords hanging from its front panel.

Figure 2.3. *Switchboard cords*

Get closer and read the names of the connections. To whom are you "energetically wired?" Are these healthy connections? Begin to pull out the cords to any unwanted old names on the switchboard. Continue until you feel one that is really charged. Ask for help from your Higher Self as you take a deep breath and yank it from the switchboard. Take the loose end that used to plug into the negative relationship and ask your Higher Self to release any negative power this cord may still have over you. Visualize the person who was at the other end. See him surrounded by the Light. Wish him well.

Ask your Higher Self to completely heal all neediness from the second chakra. Surround the entire energetic switchboard and all of its switches and relays with healing light. Visualize new light-filled fiber optic lines going out to your chosen recipients. Send the pure light of forgiveness and healing to those that need it. Hold the flow of light in your second chakra, and connect it with the light in your heart. Enjoy the feelings!

Now, go out to all the telephone lines that make up the Infosphere. Experience the waves of love and need that are flowing everywhere—without getting stuck. Feel the resonance. Visualize universal love flowing through all the wires, radiating from all the cell towers, raining down from all the satellites. Breathe goodwill to everyone.

Now, slowly become more and more aware of the sound of your breath. Leave the meditation images behind as you become more conscious of your present place and time. Make a promise to remember this experience every time you pick up a telephone receiver. Slowly open your eyes.

THIRD-LEVEL
DIGITAL DHARMA

Becoming a
Clear-Channel Broadcaster

Third-stage dharma is about our relationship to power: who has
it and who wants it, and how it's used for good or for ill. All of
these developmental issues emerged into the Infosphere with the
advent of broadcast radio.

W hile the first two chakras are energetically focused on
connections to the physical world, the middle three
levels deal with our relations to the social world. In
the domain of the Infosphere, this is the world of mass communications—radio at the third level, television at the fourth, and the
Internet at the fifth.

The energy transponder associated with third-level issues is the
hara center, the largest chakra, centered in the solar plexus. When
open and flowing, this center fuels the desire to act and powers
personal transformation. It holds the power that we need to bring

through the mastery (in Aramaic, *malkutakh*) of our vision.[1] It is from this "gut level" that we broadcast our autonomy to the world, and it is from here that our ties to family, tribe, religion, and culture and our loyalties to those whom we respect all converge.[2] When overactivated, this power center can push others away. When blocked, third-chakra energy can be unpredictable and dangerous, even violent. An underpowered third center makes one susceptible to the will of others. Matthew Fox tells us, "Our failures around the third chakra are invariably those of not coming into our strength, of yielding our strength to others, of lacking authentic outrage."[3]

The Infosphere technology that reflects the work of projecting legitimate hierarchy and respected power is the radio station. The raison d'etre of a radio station is to broadcast a powerful central signal for all to hear. This is what happens: A powerful higher frequency "carrier wave" is very slightly changed (modulated) by a speaker's voice; the modulated wave carries that imprinted message to the ears—and minds—of the world.

Radio programming (in both conventional and Internet streaming and podcast formats) reflects the third-level issues of personal versus community power, myth versus reality, our fears of separation versus our longing to belong. Radio creates a virtual place where public speech predominates: One transmitter sends out its "to whom it may concern" voice to multiple tuned and resonating receivers. Radio at its best offers the dissemination of community wisdom, mores, stories, music, and song. The dark side of this capability can bring the hypnotic shrieks and murmurings of a madman to entire nations.

Once turned on, the radio as a physical device dematerializes, in a sense, becoming a magical portal into boundless, primitive, precognitive sound-space (figure 3.1). Like the telephone, radio can sound personal and intimate, but unlike its original wireless telegraphy predecessor (whose inventors struggled for years to make it a directional, private, point-to-point medium), radio is a public, one-to-many, "broadcast" medium.[4] It provides the experience of group belonging, a sense of sharing not the anonymous space of a crowd, but a "consociate" community of like-minded thinkers sitting at the feet of the tribal storyteller or musician. Listening to the radio feels like sharing an ongoing conversation: the everyday bits of gossip, news, chants, and musical sounds that define a culture.[5]

Figure 3.1. *Radio, the voice of authority and power*

Though both the telephone and radio evoke a sense of intimacy, a crucial difference exists: Anyone can talk on the phone, but not everyone gets on the radio. The power to decide who gets to participate in radio's group talk and music-making is an issue of great social consequence. The battle over whose voices we get to hear has been part of radio's history from its inception. In the early 1920s, the early wireless pioneers broadcast without licenses. Their magical, invisible signals respected no boundaries, physical or political. Anybody could start a radio station—individual enthusiasts, newspapers, churches, department stores, schools, labor unions, radio manufacturers. In the United States, at first all broadcasters large and small shared the same two frequencies (a third was added in late 1922).

Radio's centralizing (and potentially dominating) power was recognized early on. By the late 1920s, fearing the chaos of unlicensed transmitters and unregulated speech, governments moved to limit access to the airwaves. In Europe, radio was made a government monopoly operated by the post office. In the United States, a new Federal Radio Commission (FRC) was formed, and private entrepreneurs were given licenses to operate "in the public interest, convenience, and necessity." Both forms of regulation tended to protect the establishment. In the United States, commercial interests soon overwhelmed the few stations owned by voices outside the mainstream. Networked "chain programming" from a central authoritative source soon replaced most local efforts.

Political censorship, both flagrant and subtle, characterized commercial radio from the beginning. In the United States, transmitters owned by medical quacks and religious hatemongers were shut down. At the same time the FRC also rejected the renewal applications of what it called "propaganda stations." As a result, broadcast facilities operated by educators, labor organizations, socialists, and small churches lost their prime frequencies and power levels to commercial broadcast networks. By 1937, almost ninety percent of the wattage of America's radio stations was controlled by NBC and CBS.[6]

Radio came into its full power during the dark days of the Depression and World War II. Dozens of educational radio stations

brought the world of knowledge to one-room schoolhouses and isolated farm families across rural America, teaching everything from
literature and history to touch-typing and art appreciation over the
airwaves.[7] That aspect of the era shows the medium at its third-
chakra best. However, in its shadow manifestation, this one-to-
many voice was also the perfect medium of the demagogue. For the
Germans it was Hitler; in the United States, Father Coughlin gained
huge audiences for his attacks on Roosevelt and the Jews, while
Senator Huey Long of Louisiana used radio to tout his populist
"share the wealth" campaign.[8]

Radio also suited the powerful national father figures of the
day: Roosevelt, Churchill, and Stalin used it to lead their nations out
of economic despair—and into the unifying fire of World War II.
During the war, broadcasting technology was highly controlled.
Citizens of Nazi-occupied countries could be executed for owning
a radio. Paul Levinson writes of this period:

> [Radio] messages emanating from distant strangers were taken
> into the hearts of people as if they were the words of a father
> or uncle. . . . Indeed, whether the messages were ethically right or
> not, on behalf of democracy or totalitarian control, meant to
> defend against attack or unleashing a monstrous attack on the
> innocent, did not really matter. Because the sound and impact of
> the human voice in such close, personal, quarters cut through
> and around detached rational analysis, exciting levels of emo-
> tional bonding, which, like all appeals to our adrenalin, have
> little to do with reasoning.[9]

Today access to radio is still controlled by powerful political
and commercial interests and all too often denied to the poor and
oppressed. In the shortwave bands, governments and religious ide-
ologies compete for foreign listeners, while at home, control of
broadcast radio is a major barometer of who is in control of the
machinery of state. When tanks surround a radio station, you can be
sure a military coup is in progress. From Iran to Somalia, from Haiti
to Cuba, radio and recording technologies have helped level the

playing field between small rebellions and large established states. In 2006 in Oaxaca, Mexico, protesters coordinated their takeover with their not-so-secret weapon: the radio transmitter of the shuttered university. A few decades earlier, the Ayatollah Khomeini circulated his speeches on audiocassettes, another form of one-to-many audio, as did the rebel Somali poets resisting the brutal dictator Siad Barre. These African rebels even operated a clandestine radio station from a transmitter strapped to a camel's back.[10]

Secret Radios Eyed for North Korea

Activists are planning to smuggle up to 20 million radios tuned to the Voice of America into North Korea as part of efforts to destabilize the communist regime. The campaign is aimed at giving North Koreans access to uncensored information about their own country and helping achieve regime change, Douglas Shin, a Korean-American Christian missionary involved in the campaign, said Monday. The activists, who help North Korean refugees, say they plan to smuggle the radios, which will be solar-powered, from China via boats... North Koreans face severe restrictions on their movements, and the frequencies of radios sold there are fixed to government-run broadcast stations, according to the activists.

—*Japan Times*, March 25, 2003 [11]

Radio draws its political power from its ability to tap the gut-level, third-chakra appeal of the tribal storyteller. The ages-old tradition of gathering around a powerful voice seems to be essential to the survival of cultures and appears to be "hardwired" into our brains. And radio, notes Leonard Shlain in *The Alphabet Versus the*

Goddess, is a medium of intense heroic speech. "[It is] sensuous, immediate, and very personal, like someone whispering into your ear in the dark. It can communicate nuance and intonation. Because the listener cannot *see* the speaker, radio is orality raised to the highest pitch of intensity."[12]

Marshall McLuhan understood that radio's effect is not between the ears, but in the gut. "It comes to us," he wrote, "ostensibly with person-to-person directness that is private and intimate, while in more urgent fact, it is really a subliminal echo chamber of magical power to touch remote and forgotten chords."[13] He argued it was radio that, in his words, "hotted up" the wars for independence in Africa in the 1960s.[14] Thirty years later, it was used to incite ultra-nationalism and eventually genocidal atrocities in Bosnia, Rwanda, and India.[15]

In this mode, radio can be gruesomely effective. In 1994, more than eight hundred thousand defenseless Tutsi civilians were slaughtered in Rwanda. The killers were led to their victims by the Hutu-controlled Radio Machete, which broadcast not only calls for cleansing the country of "the cockroaches," but also the locations, license plate numbers, and addresses of those targeted for extermination.[16] While satellite television and the Web are full of fundamentalist content, it is radio that calls most loudly for violent jihad in the Middle East.[17] Radio—both over-the-air and streamed over the Internet—remains the medium of choice for rallying the faithful of every faith, for using the power of disembodied voice to cultivate and motivate unseen—and unseeing—audiences.

On a less painful note, even as television has become the dominant medium, radio continues to play its role (albeit somewhat muted) as reflector of the dance of social power and group acceptance. In the developed world, radio has become a barometer of acceptance for racial and ethnic minorities. Since the Jazz Age, succeeding generations of youth have looked to radio programming to legitimize their cultural rebellions. In the late 1950s, rock and roll broke the taboos of "race music," as Elvis ("a white boy who could sing like a colored man"[18]) brought the power of rhythm and blues to America's heartland.

As television softened the heart of society towards minority communities (a process discussed in more detail in the next chapter) and replaced radio as the central focus of the living room, radio became more local, more idiosyncratic, and a little more open to once marginalized voices. In 1967 the U.S. Federal Communications Commission (FCC) began enforcing its rule that AM stations could no longer just duplicate programming on their new-tech FM transmitters. The underutilized FM band (capable of transmitting in stereo) was soon colonized as a subversive aural "underground" featuring jazz, folk music, and free-form rock, providing the soundtrack to a new generation's protests, while on the AM band, disc jockeys became the kings of the airwaves, each with a dedicated community of young followers. In Europe, young people challenged government-run radio monopolies with Beatles music transmitted from pirate FM stations aboard old freighters floating off the coast.[19]

Today, in the age of compact discs, MP3 players, pop-music ringtones, and hip-hop music made by "scratching" old vinyl records and "sampling" other's songs, the power of shared sound to create group identity endures. Contemporary hip-hop emerged from the slums of the South Bronx as the voice of dispossessed youth. By repeating "sampled" snippets of other artists' work and overlaying them with "scratches" of other musicians' tracks played back and forth, these street-party DJs created a background of sounds that was a play on aural media technology itself. Literally "claiming power" by stealing electricity from urban streetlights and housing project lobbies, the music of protest took over the streets (figure 3.2) and eventually forced its way on to the airwaves (where it was soon taken over by the forces of commerce).[20]

These identity issues are presented to us anew each morning, as broadcast radio invites us to hear our collective third-stage digital dharma as a work in progress. At its authentic best, radio brings us the sounds of our cultural identity, voices from our community, discussions with trusted friends and respected experts. It allows our second-chakra hunger for connection to be filled in the public confessional space of call-in radio. But in its shadow "ego-self" mani-

Figure 3.2. *"The True Pioneers of Hip Hop" mural,*
Monroe High School, Bronx, New York

festation, radio brings us a cacophony of screaming pundits, cynics, and hatemongers. It becomes truly the realm of the "personality"—the smut-spouting "shock jocks," the financial gurus, the astrologers and love "experts," the self-important talk-show hosts whose audience of "dittoheads" is expected to take in every word without challenge. Too much of today's "talk radio" reveals the symptoms of an overcompensating third chakra: anger, gossip, adversarial posturing, and fantasies of confrontation. On the political right, one hears blind patriotism, indignation about dissent, and harsh judgments against those outside the in-group; on the left, a righteous cacophony of aggrieved splinter groups, each talking to their own cultural niche, each certain that theirs is the only truth.[21]

This sad state of affairs is largely a result of the 1996 deregulation of the U.S. radio industry. As networks expanded to hundreds of outlets, many local voices were replaced by such domineering personalities as Howard Stern and Rush Limbaugh, broadcasting to national audiences. Radio, as our communal third chakra, was commercially transformed, in the words of *Wired* columnist Charles Mann, "from a village of small, independent stations to a bastion of the U.S. media oligopoly, content to deliver sterile, cookie-cutter broadcasts" to dwindling audiences.[22]

The domineering approach of commercial radio may, however, be its own undoing. Many listeners have responded to the predictable programming and hypercommercialization of local radio by abandoning the medium altogether and migrating to satellite and Internet radio. The former has grown in popularity by offering "narrow-cast" music and talk formats to passionate customers willing to pay $12.95 per month to hear their personal favorites and to displaced baseball fans hungry for the familiar voice of their hometown announcer. The latter has allowed small independent radio stations to find audiences around the globe; it has also made it possible for millions to go online and download their own playlists to their MP3 players.[23]

With large-scale radio so controlled and ossified, small-scale community radio projects have become the best medium for disenfranchised groups to discover their communal voice, share their common experience, and improve their governments. Community radio projects in Haiti, Latin America, and Africa empower the poor and marginalized. In the slums of Belo Horizonte, Brazil's third-largest city, Rádio Favela airs commercially shunned news and music and facilitates community activism. Created by Misael Avelino dos Santos, who started "pirate broadcasting" in 1976 and served jail time for his illegal activities, the station's advertising revenue has helped fund education programs for the mostly illiterate listeners.[24]

In Senegal, Oxfam reports that Radio Oxy-Jeunes (Oxygen for Youth)—once condemned as "a subversive group of youngsters"—now broadcasts news and discussions of such formerly taboo subjects as women's rights and AIDS in seven local languages. Similar youth-based radio programs are countering some of the same divisions created by nationalistic broadcasts. In Israel, the European Palestinian Chamber of Commerce (a nonprofit organization that publishes *The Jerusalem Times* newspaper) and the Israeli organization the Jewish-Arab Centre for Peace (Givat Haviva) are jointly sponsoring Radio All for Peace, whose mission is to provide "messages of peace, cooperation, mutual understanding, coexistence and hope."[25]

In the Guatemalan highlands in Central America, where high-powered religious stations dominate local radio, and where a Mexican businessman who lives in Miami owns the country's four main television stations and twenty-five commercial radio stations, local indigenous communities have started more than two hundred low-powered, volunteer-run, unlicensed stations. The traditional Mayan community in Chichicastenango is now organizing to secure a radio channel to broadcast in the native Quiché language. Programs will include talks about traditional healing, customs, songs, and the sacred Mayan calendars. And in northern Canada, First Nation (Native) peoples have produced award-winning programs that mix native languages with English and French translations for mainstream audiences.[26]

In the developed "first world," low-power, unlicensed "pirate" radio stations are combining "outsider" music with local news and political organizing. Thousands of these stations operate across America with ranges of up to twenty miles. Although popular among schools, religious groups, local governments, and activists, low-power broadcasting is actively opposed by the major radio and television interests. Federal lobbying by these groups has successfully erected barriers to the development of "microbroadcasting," but community activists continue to fight (legally and sometimes extra-legally) for these local voices.[27]

Whether by identification with music format or with political voice, our relationship to radio reminds us of many third-level challenges. This medium reflects all of our personal and cultural issues around power: to whom we give it, who has grabbed it from us, and where our own power center lies. Do the audio formats we surround ourselves with empower us, or do they stoke our rage? Do they educate us about leadership, or do they make us docile? Strengthening third-chakra teleconsciousness requires learning to control and modulate one's energetic broadcasts to discriminately tune in and skillfully reply only to the highest quality signals received. Once authentic power is mastered, we can graduate to the fourth-level work of the heart, finding its metaphors encoded in the flickering visual medium of television.

LIVING IN FULL THIRD-LEVEL TELECONSCIOUSNESS

The third chakra operates as a private radio transceiver, sending a person's unique signal out into the world and receiving incoming messages of the family, church, racial, and national identities that claim one's allegiance. The signals that move through this transponder are about power, but we have the dharma choice to operate either at the lower-power frequencies of ego, control, and intimidation or at the higher vibrations of autonomy, mastery, and respect.

The third chakra is where we internalize our "inner music tracks" and our personal talk show. Issues of power, self-discipline, and self-expression reside here. One who is centered in his or her personal power and open to others can broadcast confidence to all. Much more than the simple "here I am" pulse of the root chakra, this transponder encodes a complex statement of one's dreams and visions, as well as the capacity to make them real. Here is both the fire of self-discipline and the inner songs that keep us going. When we are not in balance and are fearful and uncertain of our first- or second-chakra connections, this center's output too often devolves to a distorted "boom-box" assault. In terms of its receptive qualities, a weak third chakra is easily "remote controlled" by someone else's opinions. People who are easily led by those more powerful and who take their social cues from others may have a third chakra wound from childhood, often inflicted by dominating parents or siblings. Such wounds can lead to a fear of speaking the truth or even fear of knowing what one really wants.

Much of the "cultural politics" of the last few decades has been about "finding one's voice," whether as women, gays, or members of other marginalized groups traditionally expected to keep silent.

From a dharma perspective, this step represents healthy empowerment, but overcompensation is not the answer. As a man I have learned to rekindle what author Sam Keen calls the "fire in the belly." But my men's work is also shaped by the "new warrior" creed that calls for men to transform the old paradigm of male power for domination and destruction into a "mission of service."[28] Women too, have learned to "reclaim their anger" at patriarchy, but their challenge now is to avoid being taken over by self-righteousness. For both genders, the fire of the hara center must be tempered by the loving power of the heart.

Extending the external metaphors of broadcast radio to one's dharma path allows one to ask a number of key communications questions. On the transmission side: Now that I have the microphone, how can I avoid mistaking power for mastery, volume for fidelity? On the receiving end: Whose talk shows am I listening to? What communal conversations do I absorb as my own? Am I consuming messages of autonomy and mastery, action and consequence, or am I just "cruising the dial" for outside advisors, gurus, and opinion leaders? Am I expressing my true core of being, in full, rich, multichannel stereo, or am I presenting a fake self by endlessly "looping" sampled fragments, finding my identity by expropriating and mimicking the vibes of others? Healing this center often requires "changing the channel"—or at least turning down the volume of the old tapes by focusing on a new affirmation or practice.

Autonomy—essential for personal responsibility—is built on the foundation of the first two chakras—good grounding and good relationships. A person who cannot see himself as a separate being with definable boundaries cannot fully take responsibility for his actions. When relationships are healthy, one can claim her power without fear of hurting or being hurt by others. Third-level digital dharma means carefully attending to the messages one transmits, setting one's intention on becoming a clear-channel broadcaster, radiating a wave of blessing through the web of human connectivity, trusting that it will be downloaded by those who need to hear it, trusting that it will make sense and make a difference.[29]

SUGGESTIONS FOR "RADIO YOGA"

I invite you to use the metaphor of radio as part of your digital dharma practice.

- Take some time each day to really listen to your favorite stations. If you had to describe their core values, what would they be? What would a bumper sticker version look like? Write it down and stare at it for a while. Could anyone find this statement a threat to his or her comfort? What would the bumper-sticker retorts be? Now start peeling back the slogans on each set of stickers—yours and theirs. Is there anything at the core that you have in common?

- Listen to stations that drive you crazy. What are their values? Do you share anything with them?

- Sit quietly and visualize the earth's Infosphere containing a century of radio transmissions—shortwave, long-wave, AM, FM. Absorb it all without responding. Now ask the light of your Higher Self to join with the light of all the planet's peoples to neutralize the fear-based religious or nationalist fanaticism infecting the global nervous system. Send the angry ones unconditional love; send the drowned-out voices acknowledgment.

THIRD-LEVEL TELECONSCIOUSNESS VISUALIZATIONS

Powering Up the Third-Chakra Transmitter

Wear loose-fitting clothes; have your feet bare. Alternate between drawing breath up from the center of the earth through your feet and down from the center of the universe through your crown, into your lungs. Exhale through the solar plexus.

Visualize the oxygen igniting a ball of fire at the third chakra. It becomes bright yellow and quite warm.

Begin to radiate this yellow energy outward to the world like a radio transmitter. Practice modulating the "color" (FM, frequency modulation) and the power (AM, amplitude modulation). Focus first on filling the room with this powerful energy. Expand it to encompass the building you're in with your signal, then your neighborhood, your city, and finally the whole planet. Picture thousands and then millions of other positive signals all overlapping and energizing the Infosphere with cleansing Light.

Updating Your Personal Playlist

Sit in a comfortable chair. Relax. Follow your breath to any place of tension and release it. Let go of thoughts. Allow yourself to float gently and safely away from your physical body. Feel yourself rising up to the ceiling . . . through the roof . . . up into warm, gentle clouds. Rise higher and feel the sun. Ask your Higher Self awareness to assist your intention of third-chakra healing.

Continue to drift up and away. . . . Notice the clouds thinning out and a large green forest coming into view below you. Set your intention to descend, and feel yourself slowly drifting down to a small, protected clearing in the woods. The ground is soft. You feel the warm sun on your face. You see a path back into the forest, and begin walking. Follow the path until it leads you down a flight of steps, every step bringing you closer to your third-chakra memory bank.

Follow the steps down. You notice that you are inside a building, and the stairs lead down into the basement. You can hear an electrical hum and feel the energy in the air. You see a door marked "Radio Center." You push it open and find yourself walking down a long corridor.

On your left is another door marked "Record Library." You might see shelves filled with vinyl disks or computer servers loaded with digital files. Walk down the aisle and allow one of them to call to you. Reach over and take out a disk. Hold it to your ear and "listen" (in this place, no playback devices are required).

What's the message? Is it healthy? Where was it first recorded? If you are not sure, check the label. Is it from family, friends, or religious, ethnic, or national groups?

Find your first-chakra earth connection. Build a ball of light and energy and bring it up the spark-gap transmitter at your first chakra through your solar plexus to the record you hold. If the record holds a positive message, the light will empower it. If the message is negative, the light purges the "corrupted" data tracks. Let the light do its work. Keep pulsing energy to the disk. Set your intention that the highest good will transpire. If it's an old, useless sample, let the light melt the disk and vaporize old, destructive beliefs. Discard the old "tapes" downloaded from other peoples' belief systems.

Now go to the back of the record library—there's a doorway marked "To the Heart Vault." Enter the passageway and follow it to your heart center. Feel the warmth and the light. Listen to the new music. It's there, even if it's subliminal. There's a table with a stack of new disks and MP3 files. Pick them up and carry them back to the record library. Load them into the server, write over the old files, and update the directories. Rewrite your station's playlist to reflect the enlightening new sounds!

Close the door of the record library behind you. Find yourself gently returning to the here and now. Take a few more breaths. Feel your energy, move a bit, and open your eyes to a world a bit brighter, uplifted by your internal broadcasting system repairs.

FOURTH-LEVEL
DIGITAL DHARMA

THE BROKEN HEART
OF TELEVISION

The work of third-stage digital dharma focused on "me in relation to others." At the fourth stage comes the discovery that every wave we send out ripples across other waves, creating a hologram of interfering and interrelating life stories, that the "other" we see actually reflects a part of ourselves.

While third-level work in the socio-political domain focuses on negotiating power-based relationships, fourth-level communications focuses on creating and sustaining a civic life organized on the principles of altruism and trust. At this level, interaction is about building a sense of community based on "sharing and caring." On the evolutionary spiral of global consciousness, this stage is associated with the values of the "dynamic feminine"—consensus-based decision-making, joyous cooperation, and the dream of peaceful reconciliation across the old tribal and nation-state boundaries.[1] Philosopher Duane Elgin associates this level of development with the beginning of "observer" or "witness" consciousness, the time when one learns that "one's true self extends beyond bodily desires, feelings, and mental activity."[2]

In the domain of energy yoga, fourth-level values are held at the heart chakra, the home of the Lover archetype. Indeed, this is the center that radiates our desire to fully love and be loved. As the pivot between the body and the mind, this center's work is to integrate the reality of life's limitations with our dreams of a world of unconditional love. The heart intuitively yearns for connection at the deepest levels of experience. Its greatest desire is to reveal our dreams, our joy and sadness, our beauty and light, to others. This center naturally desires to open to everyone and everything. Yet, as the Buddha taught, the world we live in is one of attachment (to the ego, to things, to the life of the body) leading to suffering, wounding, and limitation. While mystics of all faiths tell us that the blows of life awaken the heart, for most of us, openly receiving the world can easily overwhelm our capacity for both love and grief. Thus, the core challenge for this chakra is to remain, at each and every second, open and fully compassionate; its deepest shadow behaviors are rooted in its attempt to sidestep its inconsolable grief when it loses, again and again, the objects of its attachment.

When cut off from the grounding power of the lower centers, and thus uncertain of its relationship to the earth and to others, the heart center may respond by closing down and turning thick-skinned in self-defense, rejecting true intimacy in favor of the defensive strategies of intolerance and cynicism. At the other extreme, when its response is overactive hypersensitivity, fourth-chakra emotional energy can easily turn to the high drama of its shadow archetype: the Actor/Actress who is attached either to clinging codependence (always meeting the needs of others) or to the pain of the "victim syndrome" (whether focused on the never-healed "inner child" or one's aggrieved identity group).[3] More often, an unbalanced fourth chakra resorts to a combination of these responses: what Ken Wilber calls "boomeritis"—utopian dreaming and multicultural sympathies bordering on collective guilt for all the world's victims, mixed with unacknowledged attachment to luxury material goods, the acting out of grand dramas, and lack of discernment and self-discipline.[4]

Out in the Infosphere, these same polarities are held, and magnified, by the medium of television: the utopian hope for a world community, and the sad depths of dysfunctional family life. The conflicting archetypal energies of the fourth chakra seem to scream "made for TV." Fourth-level digital dharma asks us to look at this medium both as a tool of addictive consumption and as the harbinger of the enlightened global village. Television reflects both a new, compassionate "witness consciousness"—a projection of the world's desire for reconciliation and understanding—and all of the world's materialism, overstimulation, arrogance, greed, and self-pity. Television addiction starts when our deep fourth-chakra needs for loving connection are transferred into overconsumption and a delight in the humiliation of others—sometimes the self-important and self-deluded, but often the hapless, helpless, and weak. When this aspect of the medium is considered, it is no surprise that critics have called TV a "plug-in drug" that "colonizes" our minds with lies and seduction. However, let us not forget that television is also the medium through which a pioneering generation discovered the "others" who share Spaceship Earth.

Technically a television image is an interlaced mesh (figure 4.1), recreated by scanning every other line—240 of them—every sixtieth of a second. First the odd numbered lines are drawn, then the even ones, 480 in all, thirty times a second. The mind completes the half-drawn picture, filling in the missing dots line by line. Marshall McLuhan believed that the fuzzy pictures of early television drew viewers into their electronic reality by stimulating not so much sight but, above all, the emotionally powerful sense of touch. The viewer, he wrote, is constantly "filling in the spaces" in the flickering mosaic mesh, interacting with the picture tube in a creative dialog with the medium's vague and blurry images.[5] This "tactile" participation in completing the television image cuts two ways: We know on some level that the people we "see" on-screen are in fact our own mind-projections, but we also sense that we are engaging with an artificial world. Television, like many of our contemporary relationships, seems forever to be drawing us in to a half-full glass, yet leaving us thirsty for real connection.

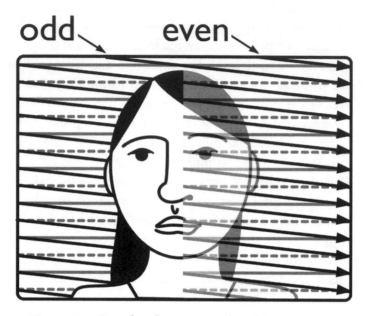

Figure 4.1. *Interlaced scanning of a television image*

Television's use of the close-up—originally necessitated by its small, low-resolution image—stimulates the fourth center's always-primed emotional energy receptors, creating instant empathy with the on-screen characters. TV's critics argue that the small screen is no substitute for the "big picture" of real life. But let's not forget that the close-up is by its nature subversive of establishment power and pretense. It reveals the human face behind the false front of the politician and "de-deifies" world leaders. Television has always challenged the establishment by its direct appeal to the fourth-chakra intelligence of its audience and by its self-reflective aware-ness that there is "more between the lines."[6]

Television favors not objective facts or reason but in-close, emo-tional involvement. Its business base may be a perfect expression of third-level "achiever energy" but its impact engages the viewer's sensitive emotional side.[7] While radio's earliest critics and promoters saw it as an extension of centralized knowledge, artistry, and political power (some predicting that there would be only one orchestra and one superuniversity left on earth), television was almost immediately recognized as a visitor that would bring the outside world and all its visual diversity into the viewer's home.

Leonard Shlain, in *The Alphabet Versus the Goddess*, tells us that it was primarily the flickering electronic hearth of television that derailed centuries of masculine linear text, bringing the return of the more feminine mode of image pattern-recognition, and with it, massive changes in social consciousness.[8] And indeed, it was television's right-brain orientation that first brought us face to face (and heart to heart) with the "foreigners" of the world—and of our own community. Despite a predominance of cowboys and Indians, violent crime shows and cartoons, TV also introduced us to outsiders who differed from us in class, gender, color, language, tribe, and nation. It connected us for the first time to the entire planet. Television, in Duane Elgin's words, "is our social witness—our vehicle for 'knowing that we know' as nations and as a human family." According to Elgin, television's coverage of the moon landing in 1969 pushed us across a developmental threshold of human awareness. For the first time we "collectively witnessed our own knowing."[9]

Paul Ray and Sherry Ruth Anderson's book *The Cultural Creatives* describes the change from the third-level (radio) culture of the 1930s, '40s, and '50s to the new fourth-level values stimulated by the explosive growth of TV in the 1960s. While Ray and Anderson only briefly mention television, they write that the big social movements of the earlier era—those associated with loudspeakers, sound trucks, and speeches on the radio, such as the union movements, the socialists, the fascists, the communists—were mostly about taking power and grabbing a share of the spoils. The movements that nurtured the first generation of the new culture—the civil rights, feminist, peace, and environmental and holistic health movements of the 1960s—were about changing our minds, changing our moral interpretation of the world.[10]

The great moments in video journalism—the marches for civil rights, the faces of hungry children and victims of war or natural disasters—all bring close emotional contact with our fellow humans. Steven Stark, in *Glued to the Set*, observes that one of the medium's first successful comedy programs, *I Love Lucy*, illustrated how television is best when it touches the emotional body:

> Because it doesn't arrive via a public sphere—like theatre or film—but comes directly into the home (the traditional domain of women), TV tends to rely on female forms of expression, such as narratives and self-disclosure. The medium's strength is going "up close and personal"; from *Person to Person* to the *Oprah Winfrey Show*, its ultimate promise has often been the disclosure of intimacy.[11]

The best television programming is about telling compassionate stories. Previously disenfranchised people and other living beings— whether the poor and homeless or endangered species such as whales and dolphins—have all found a place in TV's all-embracing portrait of the global family. Throughout the 1970s and 1980s, *Sesame Street* and the early versions of *Star Trek* embodied television's heart-softening magic, connecting us with other families, neighborhoods, cultures, and even distant galaxies. Star Trek's captains James Kirk and Jean-Luc Picard taught us how to overcome intolerance and injustice without violence,[12] Mister Rogers (figure 4.2) was there to guide families into the dark corners of childhood closets, and a generation reared on Lassie and Flipper began to insist on "dolphin-safe" tuna. (Sadly, television's open heart apparently has its limits, as PBS discovered when it aired a segment showing lesbian mothers happily raising their children—until reactionary Christian moralists had it taken off the air.[13])

Television's impact at the heart has changed how we fight our wars. The medium brings the ugliness of war "home," literally, but given television's uniquely intimate twist, it tends to humanize the enemy. In the 1970s, television coverage of the Vietnam War helped

Figure 4.2. Mister Rogers

turn the tide of public opinion against this otherwise remote conflict. Today, TV continues to subvert military victories through coverage of war's consequences for "regular citizens." In the Middle
East, coverage of Israeli and American actions by Al Jazeera, an
Arabic television network based in Doha, Qatar, has united much of
the previously factionalized Muslim world in protest—and in dangerous self-pity, the shadow side of the fourth chakra.[14] And even
Hamas, the organization responsible for dozens of suicide bomb-
ings in Israel, has itself created a "warm and fuzzy" children's television show to promote its version of Palestinian history.

The U.S. government recognized the heart-softening power of
television when it decided to "embed" reporters within fighting
units in the war in Iraq. Home-front criticism of the invasion was

dampened as journalists' heartfelt stories about the young men and women surrounding and protecting them replaced more objective reporting about "collateral damage" caused by the invasion. The horrific images of American soldiers humiliating Iraqi prisoners at Abu Ghraib Prison shown on television in the summer of 2004 did more to turn the world against the Iraq war than dozens of street protests.

In the Balkans, television is now reuniting people separated by the (radio-driven) ethnic wars of the 1990s. *Nashe Maalo*, a children's program in Macedonia, is bringing together Albanians, Turks, Roma, and Serbs. Encouraged by UNICEF, Children's Television Workshop, the creators of *Sesame Street*, produced *Rruga Sesam* (Albanian language) and *Ulica Sezam* (Serbian language) in 2004. These programs, in addition to teaching literacy and numbers, include locally produced live-action segments (developed in collaboration with both ethnic Albanian and Serbian content advisors) that emphasize respect and understanding.[15] In other parts of the former Yugoslavia, citizens are taping "video letters" to lost friends and neighbors from across the ethnic divide. The videos, recorded from dozens of locations, have been broadcast in each of the seven republics that were once one country.[16]

Television's emotional hook has its downside, however. It can ignite compassion but also seduce and beguile. "At its very best," Christian essayist David Dark tells us, "television can function as a kind of Trojan horse that ambushes our minds with the lives of individuals and cultures to whom we might not otherwise be inclined to connect ourselves." It encourages us, he says, to cultivate the quality of empathy. Yet, at the same time, it taps our most ignoble emotions, "driving us to base our identity on what we are able to purchase, hijacking our hopes with the emptiest of slogans and scenarios, and wasting our sympathies on tales that are devastatingly shallow and sentimental."[17]

Why is this? I believe that television is reflecting the heart's challenge of responding to a world of limitation, the world of the frightened ego and its ever-present personal and global "pain body."[18] Yes, it offers us real emotional connection with the fellow inhabitants of our small planet, showcasing liberal values of tolerance and self-esteem, but it also enables us to avoid experiencing all of the consequences of our actions—the suffering we ourselves cause other humans, other species, and our environment. The challenge here is to watch television from a place of psychological, emotional, and energetic open-heartedness. To achieve this kind of "clear" viewing, we must look deeply into all of the pain we hold in our own energy field and in all of mass consciousness. This is a dharma of electronic compassion. But for most of us, the challenge is too great. Without a strong grounding in the lower chakras and without the connections to the divine self held by the higher centers, the ego-mind turns away from all the painful data TV brings from the outside world and quite naturally searches for some kind of "jamming signal."

Psychologists tell us that persons reeling from the overpowering experience of true grief sometimes respond by hardening their hearts, retreating to other levels of consciousness, or translating the uncomfortable message into something less scary. The shadow side of television reflects all three of these defense strategies: avoidance, cynicism, and self-numbing addiction. We empower this industry to use all of its artistic power to cover up global grief with attention-grabbing, but essentially empty, minidramas. We self-medicate, but of course the alleged cure is often worse than the disease.

At its worst, contemporary TV programming perpetuates a kind of addictive emotionalism: The medium's potential for opening the heart has been subverted by its glorification of desire. Soap operas and reality shows offer psychological gratification at bargain closeout prices. Politics becomes spectacle, news becomes fashion reporting, and "media relations" passes for leadership. Instead of promoting real compassion, which requires a truly vulnerable heart center and can only come when one has faced one's own pain, television offers a chance to feel merely pity or disdain for the parade of losers brought to our screens, a half-response that leaves us in spiritual depression.[19]

The fourth level of the Infosphere has become a reflection of addictive personal consciousness. That world is a nightmare place where the self is defined wholly by want, wish, and the capacity to consume; where avarice, gluttony, and lust are disguised as infomercials and the pretend intimacy of the tell-it-all talk show. For many of us, stuffing ourselves with junk media and junk food has become an obsession that no diet can cure. The world of commercial television is a place where nothing interferes with desire: It is a perfect consumer society, a dream world where, as Associated Press reporter Erin Texeira puts it, "black and white kids play softball together, where biracial families e-mail photos online and where Asians and blacks dance in the same nightclub," all united by a shared love for consumer products.[20]

The presidency of Bill Clinton in many ways reflected the light and shadow of these fourth-chakra energies in the political-social sphere. He was a true television president, playing his saxophone on the late-night talk shows and appearing on MTV. His administration supported television's "green values" of civil rights at home and human rights and global connectedness abroad. He felt our pain. Yet he couldn't stop his survival-based addictive behaviors—for hamburgers, for popularity, for sexual escapade. He was a perfect baby-boomer child of the television age, undone by the emerging fifth-chakra fascination with "truth-telling" at all costs (a subject explored in the next chapter).[21]

The conflict between television's open (feminine) heart and the public's (male) fear of appearing too vulnerable[22] is being played out in the charge that television is "too liberal." Conservatives complained that during the first Gulf War, Ted Turner's cable network, CNN, showed the bombing from a too-human (fourth-chakra) level in a Baghdad hotel. Fox News, on the other hand, favored bombastic (third-chakra) invective, enhanced visual effects, and patriotic music, abandoning most of the tenets of neutral journalism to instead cheer on the military. On Fox, the hard-hearted "'Terminator' successfully replaced I-Feel-Your-Pain journalism."[23] By the time of the Iraq invasion there were three cable channels dedicated to all things military, and the most popular TV drama of 2006 featured indiscriminate torture of the most hard-hearted variety.[24]

The recent proliferation of new video channels has multiplied the number of programs both inspiring and disappointing. On the plus side, Oprah Winfrey continues to promote feminine values of service and sharing. The Discovery Channel airs numerous documentaries on the health of the planet. Even the conservative Fox network agreed to carry Morgan Spurlock's *Thirty Days*, a "reality" series featuring such empathetic situations as a homophobic military man living with a gay roommate in San Francisco and a southern Christian staying with a Muslim family—each situation lasting thirty days.[25]

But for the most part, it's more of the same self-absorption. Women's channels promise to fill the (fourth-level) heart with (second-level) music-video fantasies, sensational tell-all shows, or prime-time soaps or with (first-level) home and hearth programs. Food channels offer extreme close-ups of sensuous vegetables—"food porn"—for a society that has forgotten its connection to the soil. Men get round-the-clock soft-core sex, "extreme sports," and sensationalism disguised as "news." Meanwhile, a new generation of heartless cartoon programs such as *South Park* delivers postmodern "slacker" cynicism and juvenile dirty jokes parading as an attack against the hypocrisy of "political correctness."[26] Many of the new youth-oriented programs are, in media critic Steven Johnson's words, parasitic: "Instead of stories, we have riffs, annotations, asides . . . Beavis and Butthead, the political pundits and media watchers, the robots of Mystery Science Theater."[27] These self-referential programs are reflections of the "information glut" that now surrounds us. Their cynicism mirrors the feelings of a generation of viewers who were raised on a steady diet of television as young children and then surrounded by computers, the Internet, and video games in their teen years. Such programs reflect, as does much of the current compassion-fatigue and conservative backlash against simple liberal solutions, the failure of a television-driven worldview that was based both on naive optimism about human nature and on its mirror image, a sense of victimhood and self-pity when things don't turn out as promised.

The ungrounded heart, overwhelmed by TV-driven representations of emotional experience, can only shrug "whatever" and turn to the other chakras for support.[28] And, while many adults (along with conservative politicians and fundamentalist terrorists of every stripe) are retreating to the certainties of third-level consciousness, most young people are quite at home in the truth-testing, public-sees-all, user-created, fifth-level world of the Internet—the focus of our next chapter.

LIVING IN FULL FOURTH-LEVEL TELECONSCIOUSNESS

Television gives us a full-time opportunity to see the other as self. The embarrassing excesses of "reality" television, the advertisements promising us security through consumption, and the parade of shallow, escapist comedies can become the lenses through which we see humanity struggle with its denied and repressed responsibility for suffering in the world. We can use the medium spiritually to better perceive reality as it is, warts and all. We can hold the broken heart of humanity in compassion, without becoming stuck in our own well-worn melodramas. The flickering, incomplete mosaic can be the portal to loving mindfulness, a state where, in the words of Buddhist eco-philosopher Richard Grossinger, "instead of wanting to cache and horde, we want to share. Instead of trying to liberate only ourselves, we mean to set everyone and everything free."[29]

Perceiving that we are indeed "all one family" is the challenge of the new millennium. The global proliferation of cable and satellite TV has projected this challenge onto tens of millions of glowing screens. By revealing what we would otherwise push out of our field of vision, television can become the doorway to social and spiritual transformation. Instead of a "hundred-channel universe," might this technology enable each of us to become a channel of a hundred universes, appreciating the beauty and the imperfections in all of Creation? Will we let each retraced line remind us that we can begin again, that we can forgive those who hurt us, that we can forgive ourselves?

So let us tread gently into fourth-level dharma, imagining that we are walking on the skulls of all those enlightened souls who preceded us, and all those who will follow. Ask to be surrounded with the energy of Kuan Yin (Quan Yin), the *Bodhisattva* of Compassion, Mother Mary, Tara, all the ones who hear the cries of the world's souls and accord them unconditional mercy. Start your journey with an examination of what you consider to be your "heart-centered" relationships. The question is this: Are those relationships wrapped in codependence and attachment? Are you living the archetype of the radiant Lover, or are you avoiding vulnerability by treating love as a mental exercise? Are you grounded in spirit or full of emotions and self-pity? Or do you "love" so much that you're incapacitated by the world's pain? Many "spiritual" people take on others' sadness and think they are practicing compassion, but really they are only getting energetic indigestion from all the darkness they have swallowed.

I recently learned one of the ninety-nine names of God as known in the Islamic tradition: *Al-Tawwâb*, the Beckoner of our Return. Its companion affirmation is *Ya-Tawwâb*, which means to repent and to return to an all-loving, all-forgiving Spirit, to "bounce back" from the old stuck beliefs, to absolve others and oneself and start afresh, to be like the electron beam in the television cathode ray tube that returns to scan the screen's next line. This act of turning to the Compassionate One, and then practicing compassion with others, is taught to us by many religions. The Buddhist loving-kindness (*metta*) meditation practice asks students to focus on their intention of softening the heart and seeing others with love and understanding, realizing, in the words of Vipassana teacher Sharon Salzberg, that "just as I want to be happy, all beings want to be happy."[30] I have used the following exercises to step into the compassionate "*metta* vibration" of fourth-level digital dharma, seeing "the other" as a TV-like image of my own being. Feel free to try them.

SUGGESTIONS FOR "TV YOGA"

- **Watch commercials as tales of longing.** Ask yourself, "What unfulfilled need is this message appealing to?" Allow into your very being the true experience of the broken heart of humanity. From your heart center, emanate love to all victims of commercial exploitation, and to all beings in general.

- **Use TV to discover your heart's hidden desires and lost memories.** When you feel a deep emotional response, turn down the volume and stay with the feeling in your body. Let it become stronger. Where is it located? What is its color or sound? Ask your heart center to embrace the feeling completely. Stay with the experience for a few minutes. Ask your Higher Self to take you to the time you first felt this way. Watch the story as it plays out on your inner TV monitor. If it is painful, send forgiveness to all involved. If it is a happy moment, thank all present for giving you this gift.

- **Clear the Infosphere.** Visualize yourself joining together with others to form a field of universal love around all TV satellites. Envision Spaceship Earth being displayed on everyone's TV set all around the world. Radiate love, compassion, and forgiveness to the hearts of all who watch.

FOURTH-LEVEL TELECONSCIOUSNESS VISUALIZATION

Reediting Your Emotional Videos

This visualization starts off like the previous "radio library" healing, in which you reset your playlist. However, this time you will visit your video library and reedit the tapes that seem to drive your emotional life.

Sit in a comfortable chair. Relax. . . . Follow your breath to any place of tension in your body and release it. Let go of thoughts. Allow your awareness to float gently away from your physical body. Know that it is safe. Feel yourself rising up to the ceiling. . . . Gently move out through the roof, up into warm, gentle clouds. Rise higher and feel the sun. Ask your Higher Self and use your intention to access fourth-chakra healing.

Continue to drift up and away, moving to your left. . . . Notice the clouds thinning out and a large, green forest coming into view below you. By merely intending to descend, you feel yourself slowly drifting down to a small, protected clearing in the woods. The ground is soft. You feel the warm sun on your face. You see a path back into the forest, and you instinctively know that it is there you need to walk. Follow it until it leads you down a flight of steep steps, each one bringing you closer to your fourth-chakra memory bank.

Follow the steps down. You notice you are inside a building, and the stairs lead down to the basement. You can hear an electrical hum and feel the energy in the air. You see a door marked "Editing Suite." You open it and walk into a dimly lit hallway lined with office cubicles.

After a moment's hesitation, you notice one with your name on the door, and step inside. The room, though small, feels safe and comfortable. There is a video player (tape and digital) to your left. Straight ahead is a large TV monitor with the words "My Emotional Life" on the screen. You sit down and ask your Higher Self to assist you in reediting of one of your old "life stories."

You press "play." On the screen comes a video recreation of your story of some wound, grudge, or no-longer-needed negative belief about others. Let the scenario play out before you. Use the pause and rewind functions to isolate the old hurts. If you feel something too deeply, you can stop the show at any time. You may find it helpful to share any traumatic reruns with a therapist.

Now divide the screen into four quadrants, move your story tape into the upper left of the screen, and notice that it is labeled "My View." In the screen to the right start a tape labeled "Their View." Try seeing the view from the other person's camera.

Now open up the lower left quadrant. Ask your Higher Self to fill that part of the screen with the image of another experience that "stands behind" the person or situation that has "triggered" you in the upper scene. Maybe it's from your childhood. Maybe it's reflecting something about yourself that you haven't forgiven. Bring the energy of forgiveness to your story. You can say the words, "I forgive you (and myself) and release the past."

Create a similar story under the other person's screen, in the lower right quadrant. It doesn't matter if what appears is "true" or not. It's all about the stories we play back over and over again. Send this fellow human deep love and understanding for the pain that caused him or her to hurt you.

Bring in the power of universal love to reedit these clips with an alternative ending. Send the pain in each screen to the Light, replacing it with compassion for the human condition. Forgive yourself for the resulting "drama." Ask your Higher Self to empower your Lover qualities and protect you from the negativity and fear of others. Open your heart center to the force of universal love.

FIFTH-LEVEL
DIGITAL DHARMA

LIVING IN TRUTH ON
THE WORLD WIDE WEB

While television offers an invitation to look at a multicultural world, it is still a world "out there." Fifth-level digital dharma, on the other hand, is about actually connecting with all the various "others"—the peoples and cultures—that share this planet, and with all of creation. We move from observing the ripples of the hologram to the understanding that we are all part of the same reality, that one action affects the entire creation.

On the path of the chakras, fifth-level dharma challenges are held at the throat center, the transponder of cosmic sound, self-expression, and creativity. This center's core issue is communication itself, and its demon is falsehood. Positive fifth-chakra energy can be found in the free flow of information and creative ideas within and among small, trusted groups such as fellow worshippers, service volunteers, and support and recovery circles. Its shadow can be found in cults of all kinds and in a world where every communications technology is enlisted in the cause of making money or promoting the false self.

In the social domain, this new dharma asks us to make a radical jump into what the authors of *Spiral Dynamics* call "second-tier thinking"—the stage of consciousness where one is aware of both the interior dimensions of development and the exterior "big picture" of the overall spiral of existence. Second-tier thinking, in Ken Wilber's words, "is instrumental in moving from relativism to holism, or from *pluralism* to *integralism.*"[1] Here, one lives in multiple overlapping and integrative networks; here, the other is found everywhere, a reminder that one is a part of "a commons" much larger than one's family, nation, or culture. At this stage of spiritual evolution, communications centers on ideas themselves. At its most positive, fifth-level consciousness begins to become aware of itself and intuitively seeks its source across all religions and teachings: At this level, life is for learning.[2]

Whatever one's position on whether all of humanity will succeed in making "the second-tier shift,"[3] fifth-level digital dharma urges us to speak truthfully and act in ways that cause no harm to the fabric of life. For in a world of instant, unfiltered connectivity, even small "private" actions often have large systemic consequences. On the receiving side, the equivalent challenge is learning how to remain present to, but not swayed by, all the messages—electronic and physical—that bombard awareness. As our culture expands into interconnected modes of communications, fourth-level utopianism begins to confront the reality that not everyone is "nice" and that "out in the real world" one must protect oneself from being taken advantage of. Expertise and one's reputation for truthfulness begin to determine one's power in this new environment.

A strong fifth chakra is a "truth filter"—the Warrior's shield that protects the Lover's heart from lies and illusion. The sign of an underdeveloped (and thus overwhelmed and "broken open") fifth chakra is an excessive focus on the "presentation of self" that takes the form of nonstop talking (with little real content), poor listening, and outright lying. When this center shuts down in self-

> Our throat is the center of truth; as it is where we can either speak truth or lies. It is also the energy center associated with choice. Every choice that we make either takes us closer to our truest self or farther from it. This chakra teaches us the classic lesson of "cause and effect" or, said in another way, "karma." When the choices we make are in line with our truest self, our fifth chakra is healthy, and we become charismatic, powerful and at peace.
>
> —Mike Stokes, Freedom Yoga[4]

defense, all creativity is blocked. At a personal level, this blockage is manifested as cynicism and depression. Out in cultural space, the blockage becomes the overly intellectual side of deconstructionism, where, in the analysis of every hidden assumption, idea, and social structure behind any attempted communication, nothing is accepted as true, all values are transient, and what remains consists only of fleeting figments of clashing subcultures and languages.

All of the light and shadow of fifth-level digital dharma is held and then reflected back to us by the net of instantaneous connectivity, overlapping voices, online communities, shining jewels, and shifting realities that is the Internet. This is a virtual "place" where such conventional limitations as time and space are gone forever, along with previously assumed distinctions between self and other.[5] While the mass media of radio and television bombard us with images and sounds, they do not demand much of us other than our attention and our commitment to consumption. The Internet, on the other hand, offers both instant "surfing" for fleeting stimulation and an opportunity to connect deeply and cocreatively with other souls. It is the medium of a new generation, and it (along with the digital media described in the next chapter) has shaped the worldview of that generation no less than television did for the "boomer" generation.

Far away in the heavenly abode of the great god Indra, there is a wonderful net which has been hung by some cunning artificer in such a manner that it stretches out indefinitely in all directions. In accordance with the extravagant tastes of deities, the artificer has hung a single glittering jewel at the net's every node, and since the net itself is infinite in dimension, the jewels are infinite in number.

There hang the jewels, glittering like stars of the first magnitude, a wonderful sight to behold. If we now arbitrarily select one of these jewels for inspection and look closely at it, we will discover that in its polished surface there are reflected all the other jewels in the net, infinite in number. Not only that, but each of the jewels reflected in the one jewel is also reflecting all the other jewels, so that the process of reflection is infinite.

—The *Avatamsaka Sutra* of Hua-Yen Buddhism[6]

On the radio, one has to fight to get to a microphone; on the Web, access is far less of an issue. Now the challenge is ensuring that your voice won't be lost in the simultaneous broadcast of a billion other streams and podcasts. Television prods us to open our hearts to the world; the Internet reflects the fifth-level challenge of dealing with the consequences of such openness. "Always-on" network connections have thrown us head-first into a sea of memes—idea fragments that flow from brain to brain, reproducing like viruses, so that the Net's constant chatter inevitably mimics the babble and distraction of our planetary "monkey mind." We are discovering the hard way that living with such an information glut without adequate "boundary protection" can be dangerous. In the words of critic John Lahr, "we know too much and too little; the world is at once too close and too far away."[7]

A number of writers have focused on cyberspace as the new frontier for the reemergence of a previously suppressed spirituality, hoping that somewhere out in cyberspace is a portal to the divine. Others see the Web as an antihuman, mental-abstract space for the playing out of age-old apocalyptic visions: what author and critic Michael Grosso calls "the technocalypse project."[8] In reality, the Infosphere carries both of these energies. The Internet is a social space beyond the laws of physics, an immaterial "place" not just of disembodied thought, but also of creativity and the emergence of new cultural memes. I believe that the core challenge associated with living in this always-connected global brain can only be met by the practice of active discernment. On the Net, where all traditional metrics of identity and physical reality no longer apply, we can enjoy newfound freedom from the old constraints on what we can say, read, listen to, or view, but we also need to learn to distinguish between voices of truth and the songs of illusion.

> When I "go" into cyberspace I leave behind both Newton's and Einstein's laws. Here, neither mechanistic, or relativistic, or quantum laws apply. Traveling from Web site to Web site, my "motion" cannot be described by any dynamical equations. The arena in which I find myself online cannot be quantified by *any* physical metric; my journeys there cannot be measured by *any* physical ruler.
>
> —Margaret Wertheim,
> *The Pearly Gates of Cyberspace*[9]

The very architecture of the Internet fosters ambiguity and unpredictability. Because the original design challenge behind the Internet was to provide a communications network that could withstand a nuclear attack and the destruction of traditional switching centers, there is no control "center" or manager for the Net's millions of interconnected subnetworks of routers and servers. Unlike traditional (analog) telephone company "circuit switching," which is based on a direct, dedicated path between sender and receiver, the Internet chops messages up into tiny digital "packets" and sends them out to find their own way through the system to their intended destination (figure 5.1).

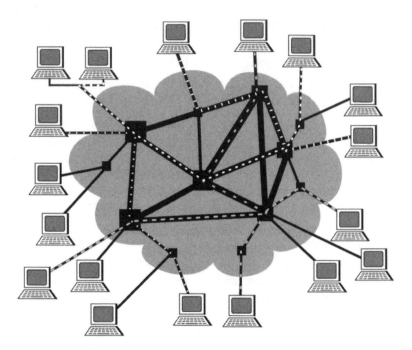

Figure 5.1. *Packet network routing map*

Each Internet data packet carries both a header and a tail section in addition to the information "payload." The header includes the destination address and the sequence number of the information data segment inside the packet "envelope." The tail carries error-checking information. Once sent out on the Net, each packet is "free" to take a different path, going from network router to network router, each time asking the router to pass it on to the next node that might be either closer to its desired destination or relatively free of competing traffic. Packets carrying different parts of the same message (where "message" can mean text, photo, audio, or video content) often take different routes, getting redirected around heavy traffic, to reach their final destination. Only at the end of the road are all the packets assembled into the correct order, allowing the true meaning of the entire message to emerge.[10]

Unlike the well-regulated space of radio and television, the World Wide Web is still a neutral and relatively open frontier. Even so, many governments still attempt to censor public chat rooms and limit access to "dangerous" sites, and the U.S. government has started its own Constitutionally questionable "data mining" programs to sniff out child pornographers and potential terrorists.[11] However, despite the efforts of repressive governments and monopolistic corporations, no one state or organization can fully control the world's electronic conversation. From Tibet to Burma, China to Zimbabwe, from indigenous communities in the Yucatan to the Cyber PowWow of the Mohawk Nation, easy access to this space has given the most powerless and invisible victims of human rights abuse and government tyranny a voice. As the *New York Times* human rights columnist (and 2006 Pulitzer Prize winner) Nicholas D. Kristof observes, the Chinese Communist Party won at Tiananmen Square, but now "it's the Chinese leadership itself that is digging the Communist Party's grave, by giving the Chinese people broadband."[12]

The Internet has allowed formerly marginalized peoples to connect and claim their place in the spectrum of human communications. It has fostered vibrant yet decentralized online communities based on unique interests, no matter how personal or idiosyncratic those interests are. This democratization of access has turned the old "passive audience" model of media consumption on its head, especially given the near-instantaneous emergence of more than 55 million (as of October 2006) user-created blogs (short for "Web logs") and more podcast feeds than the total number of radio stations in the world, with more coming online by the minute.[13] Television viewing and radio listening is rapidly declining as more people, especially in the commercially powerful 18- to 49-year-old demographic, discover the power to choose and share media content over such channels as iTunes and YouTube. New businesses have emerged, and old business models are being seriously challenged; intellectual property rights are being compromised, while at the same time millions of new "content providers" are finding a platform for their messages and a place to influence contemporary culture and politics.[14]

For example, world music shared over the Net mixes and matches genres and musical styles across cultures. This exchange has helped counter the mass media's homogenization of markets and inspired creative mutual interdependence based on peer-to-peer relationships. The community vision of the World Wide Web offers us a glimpse of what Buddhist scholar Enrique Dussel calls transmodernity: "the emergence of voices from the four quadrants of the Earth calling for mutual interdependence of resources and human rights, ecological justice, and a new collective consciousness."[15] The growth of the environmental movement, our awareness of global warming, the creation of virtual support groups of every kind, and the assimilation of holistic health and Eastern spiritual systems are examples of the new "Internet consciousness."[16]

The Internet is becoming the world's first global library, where every word on every Web page (and eventually every published book) will be, according to *Wired* magazine's "senior maverick" Kevin Kelly, "cross-linked, clustered, cited, extracted, indexed, analyzed, annotated, remixed, reassembled and woven deeper into the culture than ever before."[17] The Internet has already liberated a new alternative press and scores of antiauthoritarian political commentators. By posting alternative views, Web reporters (and citizen whistle-blowers) are challenging government "news management" strategies. Grassroots independent producers are rejecting the hierarchical, distributor-controlled models of theatrical and television release in favor of posting their work directly on their personal video blogs. Even idiosyncratic amateur footage is being shared among friends—and more often with strangers—over the Net. One Missouri man's minitravelogs on his Amtrak trips got more than

10,000 views in two weeks.[18] The coupling of the digital camera and cellphone (and now the cellphone with integrated video camera) to the Internet has made photojournalists and crime-watch detectives out of everyone.[19]

On the downside, the Internet is replete with scoundrels and shady places, as most of the human race is far from second-tier development. Reflected in the Infosphere are all the symptoms of a dangerously overactive fifth chakra: self-righteous speech that is often "arrogant, dogmatic, gossipy, domineering, over-reactive, hyperactive, and/or fanatical."[20] This unfiltered network gives equal voice to hatemongers, liars, and unscrupulous profiteers capitalizing on our fear-based impulses. Cyber-criminals (usually young men given free access to fifth-level tools while still in their second and third stages of emotional development) release rapidly spreading, destructive computer viruses. Every Internet user faces a tidal wave of distraction, from pornography to the "blogosphere," that looms just a few mouse clicks away. For every online utopian community, there's another full of second-chakra seductions or third-chakra anger. The Web has made instant pundits out of rumormongers and facilitated the dissemination of violent terrorist tactics to followers across the planet.[21]

Despite all the hype of the "new Internet economy," few firms (aside from marketers such as eBay and Amazon and search tools such as Google) actually make much money over the Net. The ones that do appear to have their roots in our lower-chakra shadows, turning parts of the Net, in *Wired* editor Bruce Sterling's view, into a pit of spam and swindles, pornography, corporate advertising, and government surveillance.[22] This tendency is nothing new: Hermes, the herald of the gods, the inventor of the lyre, the god of communications and public speaking, is also known as a thief and trickster. Homer could have been describing much of the Internet when he wrote of Hermes that he was "a bringer of dreams, a watcher by night, [and] a thief at the gates."[23]

The Internet is a technology whose gift is to show us all the ways that we—and our entire society—hide our light through secrecy and lies. It has thrown open every "closet" of human behavior and moved us beyond the excuse of denial, making us privy to everything from the bad behavior of college sports heroes and the sexual strayings of spouses and presidents, to hidden fraternity hazing practices and horrific prisoner abuse by our own soldiers.[24] The sweep of such revelations touches unexpected corners of our culture. Once-secret religious doctrines, practices, and mystical texts are now available to all. According to a recent news report, "husbands and wives, moms and dads, even neighbors and friends increasingly are succumbing to the temptation to snoop," using inexpensive keystroke recording software to track their partner's (often now, their ex-partner's) e-mails. Funeral directors now have to screen online guest books for posts from disgruntled family members, mistresses, and coworkers that "diss the dead," or reveal, through postings such as "I met the deceased at an AA meeting," more than the family might wish to know. Because of Internet postings, professional wrestling has been revealed to be a scripted soap opera in tights, and even online "bookies" are finding that their Web-savvy clients now know more about the odds than they do.[25]

As David Weinberger, coauthor of *The Cluetrain Manifesto*, observes, "hyperlinked organizations never met a wall they liked."[26] And, as William Gibson points out, the Internet's very "nakedness" has a positive side: Scrutiny is no longer the exclusive tool of governments and powerful employers but has become democratized. No one can keep a secret for long. "In the age of the leak and the blog, of evidence extraction and link discovery, truths will . . . be outed, later if not sooner."[27] Running parallel with the emerging world of Big Brother surveillance (thousands of public sites are monitored by television cameras in New York City and London) is the phenomenon of Little Brother with his digital camera holding the state—or the establishment media—accountable. The Internet has shown us videos of everything from the returning coffins of the Iraqi war dead, to the latest brutality of the Los Angeles Police Department, to the New York City sanitation worker who was caught by a security camera breaking glass in front of a store so that he could write the owner a bogus $300 ticket.[28]

> The networks aren't interested unless it will attract millions of dollars in advertising revenue. Meanwhile, there are people and events all around us that are meaningful and that people would love to watch.
>
> — Lisa Rein, San Francisco–based
> Internet video journalist [29]

Web-based citizen documentation regularly thwarts information control by the powerful. The Pentagon is in a quandary about soldiers' blogs originating from Iraq. As the *Washington Post* reported in August 2005, journalists are no longer the only pipeline to the front. In today's war in Iraq, "service members themselves are delivering real-time dispatches—in their own words—often to an audience of thousands." [30] "A lone individual," writes *Wired* contributing editor Dan Pink, "can now monitor a large institution and transmit the pictures to the entire planet." [31] And, at the same time, satellite photo images of any place or structure on the planet are now available for all to see—often over the objections of the building owner or the local government—with a few clicks on Google Earth. [32]

More and more "subjects" of television interviews are responding to what they perceive as biased reporting by posting their own videos, transcripts, or other documentation on their personal Web sites, creating alternate versions of the "truth." The traditional one-way interview is morphing into a repository of edited and unedited content, including reporters' notes and e-mail exchanges between journalist and subject. [33] Even blog readers are being asked to become investigative reporters, checking out story leads fed to them by online journalists.

On the shadow side, the Internet reminds us of all the ways people already use technology to hide the truth. Our mass media is saturated with "reality shows" and "creative nonfiction" of dubious authenticity. Counterfeit global branding "makes it easy to create fake products with broad appeal on someone else's promotional dime."[34] And then there's the saga of "lonelygirl15," a "fifteen-year-old" who became one of the most popular video-bloggers on You-Tube: She turned out to be an eighteen-year-old film-school graduate whose angst was scripted by a pair of twenty-seven-year-olds and whose online mail was answered by the wife of the producers' lawyer. When the Internet is used to bend the truth, isn't it just reflecting a society where the disastrous financial condition of the infamously bankrupt Enron Corporation is hidden in an obscure footnote; where priests turn out to be pedophiles; and where presidential critics are mocked for living in the "reality-based community"?

For some, the formal resemblance between the Hua-yen vision [of Indra's net] and our planetary trellis of fiber-optic cables, modems, microwaves, screens and servers suggests that, in a symbolic sense at least, we may now be hardwiring a network of connections that reflects the nondual interdependence of all reality. . . . The net of Indra works its real magic by dissolving our habitual tendencies to divide the world into separate and autonomous zones: inside and out, self and other, online and off-, machines and nature. So the next time you peer into the open window of a Web browser, you might ask yourself: "Where does 'the network' end?"

—Erik Davis, *TechGnosis*[35]

Yes, surfing the Internet can put you face-to-face with the uglier side of humankind. The equivalent of "road rage" channeled into harassment and electronic vendettas, disgruntled "ex's" turning into stalkers, predators in chat rooms, online identity theft, hate sites, and the proliferation of viruses and spam—these are just a few examples of Internet ugliness. Because the Net cannot be censored effectively, it forces us to ask the hard question: Where is the truth when everyone can say anything they want?

As cyber-teens exercise their newfound freedom of expression online, adolescent bullying has migrated from the schoolyard to the virtual world, taking on new forms. Some of the new weapons in the "teenage arsenal of social cruelty," according to an August 2004 *New York Times* report, include screen-name theft, slander, phony and scandalous e-mail, and massive invasions of privacy. More troubling than online bullying is the flourishing teen porn cyber-underground, run by teenagers who expose their most intimate selves, performing before hundreds of adult "fans," using inexpensive Webcams and instant messaging software.[36]

Unfortunately, malicious viruses, worms, spyware, and spam have compromised a network built by academics and designed for the freest flow of information. Most Internet users are, according to a recent University of Pennsylvania study, "pitifully green" about cyber-security. Black-market "phishing" scams that steal credit card numbers from naive victims have become a sad fact of life.[37] The lesson of this compromised Web space is the need for discriminating awareness online, as in life: Truth is not a mass-market commodity; openness may be taken for weakness. Cyber-security words such as alias account and proxy server play on fifth-level identity issues, while the presence of defensive firewalls illustrates the need for vigilance against those who present a false outer self.[38] As Internet access evolves from wired to wireless connections, the number of users attacked by hackers is skyrocketing. Here's one nightmare scenario that has already happened: Innocent citizens return home to find the FBI investigating how their unprotected wireless home connection was used to upload pornography, stolen credit card data, and other illegal material from a car parked outside the house.[39] The experience of vulnerability online is reminiscent of the anxiety that McLuhan identified as a response to the first (telegraphic) networks. Indeed, the potential threats from our global high-speed digital version are more real. Erik Davis reminds us that "mystical reports to the contrary, it seems that the realization that 'everything affects everything all the time' is not always such a great release."[40]

> Anyway, sometimes when I connect to the Internet I sit there, wondering exactly what I am doing. . . . I feel as if I could just ask the right question to a search engine I could find the truth on the Internet. Not just a truth, but The Truth. I do try sometimes; mostly on ask.com. I put in questions such as "what is the meaning of life?" which ask.com doesn't even try to answer or "why am I here?" to which ask.com responds with a site titled "food for worms."
>
> —"Persephone," in blog journal "A Statue Turned Its Head"[41]

Pondering the immense social impact of Internet connectivity presents parallel lessons for one's personal inner life. Fifth-level dharma asks us to live with a transparent heart in an overwhelmingly diverse world. This manner of living requires appropriate energetic filters to keep out unwanted negative signals—just as in the electronic world we have our TiVos and caller ID, air filters, the V–Chip, noise-canceling headphones, and iPods.[42] In a world where "transparency" brings not the one big truth, but in Gibson's words, "deliriously multiple viewpoints, shot through with misinformation, disinformation, conspiracy theories and a quotidian degree of madness," we need to cultivate the fifth-chakra power of discernment.[43] On the Internet as in all communications, appropriate and healthy interfaces between medium and message—between the expanding universe of information producers and one's inner consciousness—are required. This means practicing the Buddhist art of mindfulness: both conscious attention and conscious *in*attention.

On a deeper level, the Internet suggests that fully empowered fifth-chakra teleconsciousness requires more than just good defenses: It requires trust. Simply building bigger firewalls against cyber-spies and junk content does not bring real security. Despite all the best "computer locking" software, most determined teens can easily find a porn site or two or a hundred. In an interconnected global net-work, the old "border patrol" approach no longer protects us from foreign attacks—particularly when the "foreigners" have already infiltrated the territory, and they look just like us! According to many Web security experts, the best defense is actually more trans-parency, more and better ways to verify the truth. To that end, new software and protocols are under development that will enable us to verify our online sources.[44]

Principles of the Attention Trust

Property: You own your attention and can store it wher-ever you wish. You have CONTROL.

Mobility: You can securely move your attention wherev-er you want whenever you want to. You have the ability to TRANSFER your attention.

Economy: You can pay attention to whomever you wish and receive value in return. Your attention has WORTH.

Transparency: You can see exactly how your attention is being used. You can DECIDE who you trust.

—The Attention Trust, from http://www.attentiontrust.org

A new factor in this landscape is the peer-to-peer (P2P) net-work, in which computers link directly to other computers without going through any central controller (figure 5.2). As P2P becomes the dominant way to exchange music, video, personal audio, and photos, as well as critical business information and research data, new ways of establishing trusting relationships are emerging. Overcoming the challenge of authentication and integrity are criti-cal to the reliability of such open systems.

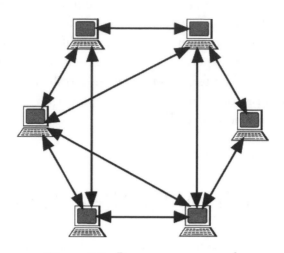

Figure 5.2. Peer-to-peer network

Traditional approaches to this problem have focused on elabo-
rate authentication and encryption systems. As Andy Oram, an editor at O'Reilly Media, writes:

> The traditional Internet has been trying to solve the authentica-
> tion problem for decades, by which I mean: Internet developers
> want to create a worldwide security system that lets you negoti-
> ate a contract for millions of dollars, digitally sign a contract, and
> feel that you're on just as solid ground legally as if you'd sat in a
> lawyer's penthouse and signed papers with the president of the
> partnering corporation. Well, bottom line is: we don't have that
> system. And the path pursued by the current security commun-
> ity isn't getting us there.[45]

Peer-to-peer networks are even more prone to security breaches. As
a result, their designers have turned to a more community-based
verification system: a web of trust. Many of these sharing networks
are membership-based, so-called "darknets" where users "get access
only through established relationships" and only by invitation.[46] In

the Internet community, as Bruce Schneier observes, "knowing the neighbors is more important than knowing karate." As the *New York Times* reports, trusting-peer-based programs such as Bittorent (created by "Robin Hood geeks") are "replacing centrally-managed commercial providers, with their odious spyware, advertising and copyright charges."[47]

New search engines are being designed around "respect models"; these engines combine geographic proximity with subject-matter relevance and test a recommendation against the shared values of others in your social network. Yahoo has launched "MyRank," a service that "organizes pages based on how closely search users are related to one another in their social network and on their reputation for turning up helpful information." It deals with the problem of search engine manipulation by "using a collection of human eyes and minds to sort the wheat from the chaff."[48] Another company offers a search service that "returns content published by people that have a relationship with the person searching." This assumes that friends (or friends of friends) might be more trusted than a casual work acquaintance and might be more willing to discuss their movie, product, or destination rankings than a stranger might be.[49] Google, responding to this social-ranking challenge, has added a feature to its satellite image database allowing users to annotate maps and share them within their communities.[50]

In today's information economy, businesses can no longer operate as insulated fiefdoms. They must share vital data with partners, suppliers, and customers through overlapping networks based on trust. Integration is no longer focused vertically, within the organization and its affiliates, but horizontally, across what technology commentator Michel Bauwens calls "vast webs of inter-company co-operation." These same networks, according to Bauwens, open businesses to a more "politicized" consumer who can, "withhold his/her buying power with an internet and blogosphere able to destroy corporate images and branding in the very short term through viral explosions of critique and discontent."[51] Cyber-citizen activism can also be constructive and even vital to modern businesses. eBay facilitates more than a billion person-to-person online auctions every year; its chief guarantee of integrity is user-generated ratings—over three billion of them to date![52]

As to the vast amounts of personal data held by our telephone companies and online providers, given the unwillingness of these companies to purge this valuable customer data (or say "no" to warrantless government snooping), our only protection is a company's reputation for telling the truth and respecting its customers' privacy. Even once-expunged court records (the "clean slate" granted by a judge for minor convictions years ago) are finding their way on to the Web, as "records once held only in paper form by law enforcement agencies, courts and corrections departments are now routinely digitized and sold in bulk to the private sector."[53] "Cyberprivacy" is an oxymoron in a free-access world of interlinked databases and surveillance systems, where commercial programs routinely collect information about online searches and e-mail topics of interest to advertisers, the government, and the neighbors. We are all "data naked" when every Web-based transaction, every credit card purchase, every trip through the grocery store, and every phone call (and its originating location) is now "on the record."[54]

Young people, raised by television to see everything as media presentation, have embraced the fifth-level tools of blogging, video-sharing, and social networking (conducted on such sites as YouTube, Facebook, and MySpace) as their primary modes of self-expression. They create their own page designs; post pictures of family, friends, and admired media figures; share poetry and their own art. They post the music (and music videos) they are drawn to, and they "friend" each other by creating links from their pages to newfound buddies, who in turn connect them to their friends.[55]

For the Internet generation, the "other" is not to be feared or conquered, nor observed as a mirror of self, but simply communicated with—even if it's a television program, movie, cellphone company, or deodorant.[56] People of this generation see themselves as citizens of the world, and they are quite comfortable volunteering their innermost fears and fantasies, making confessions, or rating their lovers for the world to see. Reflecting youthful optimism and naiveté, they have no thought for how today's pictures and confessions will look tomorrow—or two or three years later—at that critical job interview.[57]

Cyber-networking has also spawned entire communities based on the uncanny "six degrees of separation" phenomenon: "my friends know people who know people who can help me, who might possibly become my friends."[58] At the end of 2006, MySpace had more than 100 million users and more than twice as many visitors as Google. Friendster.com started the online "social networking" trend by connecting its millions of users to the "friends of their friends." Of course, this hasn't stopped more than 8,000 "pretendsters" (or "fakesters") from capitalizing on these services, including dozens of authors looking to boost sales of their own books with fake rave reviews. On MySpace, one investigator found a few hundred registered sex offenders, while other users have apparently "padded" their pages with rented images of good-looking models.[59]

Today, "word-of-mouse advertising" has become more important for many Web businesses than traditional TV advertising.[60] Music, books, and films that would never reach more than a few hundred buyers get discovered on Rhapsody, Amazon, or Netflix through the multiplying power of human recommendations, plus smart software that can tell you, "If you liked that, you might also want to try this." The nearly unlimited storage capacity of the Net allows whole new audiences to develop around unique interests. In the words of *Wired* editor Chris Anderson, "What matters is not . . . how many [customers] are seeking a particular title, but only that some number of them exist, anywhere."[61]

Even as big portions of the Internet are filled with junk and shadow, every day new jewels are also being created. The trick is having the fifth-level tools to find them, while filtering out the rest. These tools are the key to ferreting out the diamonds in what Anderson terms the "long tail"—the eighty percent of the nonbestseller backlist that never finds its way onto the shelves of traditional brick-and-mortar retailers. In his recent book *The Long Tail*, Anderson describes the flow of filtering systems that take a user of the Rhapsody music site from a bestseller list in a particular subgenre, through a pattern-matching selection of "related artists," to an editor-created list of followers of a particular band's style, to a collaboratively filtered stream of songs by bands favored by those who have purchased recordings or downloads of the band the user may have originally selected. Just a few clicks can lead a user to an album far from his or her original limited expectation. In long-tail markets, where everything is eventually available, recommendations based on tracking thousands of other customer experiences and product ratings will become the selection tool of choice.[62]

On the political front, Howard Dean's successful use of the Web to activate his supporters and raise unprecedented amounts of campaign funds (in small donations) was based on "meet up" software that brings together like-minded people in trusted circles of friends. Moveon.org used similar software to organize everything from door-to-door canvassing to neighborhood potluck dinners and phone-calling parties during the 2004 and 2006 national elections. Clearly, the lesson (in Infosphere terms) is that the fifth-level ingredient of reputation is essential. It is measured not in the volume of the transmission (third chakra) or one's ability to tell a compelling story (fourth chakra), but in the respect earned from others by sharing one's gifts, whether that be expertise, objects (physical or virtual), opinions, or computing cycles. The "golden side" of the Internet is driven by what Kevin Kelly calls "the electricity of participation." Old property- and contract-based models of production will require new cooperative, trust-based relationships.[63]

Gifting Technologies and the Web

There are many online communities with gifting as a central characteristic: newsgroups, Web logging ("blogging"), file sharing, and other donated digital and computational resources. In fact, the Internet was initially characterized by a great deal of volunteer effort and "community spirit:" participants shared advice, technical support, and the like. One could even argue that since there was so little to get in the early days of the Web, much of its initial development was driven by people who wanted, for various reasons, to gift.

The categories of what people gift online can also be very revealing.

Expertise. Perhaps the most common example of online gifting is in the form of expertise, broadly defined. This has been the subject of discussion since the earliest days of the Internet. This is made even more significant by the fact that posting (or contributing) something to online forums is not always trivial; there are often many social and technical conventions, requirements, and restrictions. Even more, people who volunteer to moderate discussions often do so in the face of great hostility, constant criticism, and very little gratitude. In addition to expertise that is directly responsive to individual requests, there are a great number of Web sites with free medical advice, consumer reports, technical support, travel updates, and the like.

Artifacts. The current file-sharing phenomenon centers largely on digital artifacts, such as music, books, movies, and software. Although this is the focus of current controversy, it is important to remember that the exchange of many digital goods does not violate any existing copyright law. Many goods are no longer under copyright—or were created (or subsequently released from traditional copyright restrictions) specifically with the intent that they be freely available. There are a number of services appearing to facilitate the gifting of physical artifacts. Book Crossing [http://www.bookcrossing.com/], for example, is a free online service that combines the Web and messaging to allow participants to notify other participants that they have finished reading a good book and left it in a specific public location—and providing information about the nature and location of the book.

Storage and bandwidth. There are a number of projects based on users donating unused resources from their networked machines. To mention just two examples of projects that make use of "spare bandwidth or cpu cycles," there is the SETI@Home project [http://setiath ome.ssl.berkeley.edu/] which provides a screen saver that allows a host computer to devote processing cycles to the analysis of data. Similarly, Radio Free Virgin, a streaming music service, uses a technology to allow participants to redistribute (re-stream) the music stream to other computers connected to the Internet. As an example of gifting storage, many universities, foundations, and individuals donate space on their computers to make publicly and freely available different resources.

—Kevin McGee and Jörgen Skågeby[64]

Third-chakra-driven styles of "broadcasting one's expertise" are giving way to new fifth-level "communities of knowledge," with blurred boundaries between authority and audience. University lecturers and conference speakers, for example, now face audiences wirelessly connected to their own expert sources—and each other. The result is that the traditional post-lecture "back-channel" responses have moved from the corridor into the auditorium. One crusading technology conference blogger invented a "hecklebot," a text display device that faces the speaker and displays real-time (and often critical) responses from what the *New York Times* called "the

Geek Chorus," that is, audience members acting as on-site fact checkers.[65]

Spiritual groups as well are using peer-to-peer communications to upend traditional hierarchical power structures. The hypocrisy of the glorified guru, preaching transcendence while bedding his students and accumulating Rolls Royces, is now public "blog fodder." Michel Bauwens (in his "P2P" blog) reports about group cyber-meditation sessions, where egalitarian-minded spiritual searchers, "collectively experiment and confront their experiences," anticipating what John Heron calls a new "participatory vision of human spirituality."[66] The explosive success of some of the largest evangelical churches in the United States has been linked to networking "lots of little church cells—exclusive, tightly knit groups of six or seven who meet in one another's homes during the week to worship and pray." These groups are in turn networked together into the larger church community.[67]

Of course, all of this heady freedom to communicate and share has its downside. As multiple truths flood the Infosphere, the fanaticism of those who believe in the certainty of one and only one truth has taken a bloody turn for the worse. A deadly combination of radical fundamentalism, rage, and immature third-level consciousness has allowed some self-reinforcing communities of true believers to coordinate and document their terrorist campaigns online. Osama bin Laden and al-Qaeda have created their own versions of "Friendster" with cells in cities all over the world. Impressionable and angry young Muslims can be recruited from the ranks of self-contained online *jihadi* forums and self-referencing chat rooms into what Howard Bloom calls a "complex distributed conspiracy . . . brought to us courtesy of the World Wide Web and the cellphone." Warfare itself has followed the Internet model, as informally joined networks of stateless cells, coordinated by high-tech communications, engage the structured armies of the old order.[68]

As fifth-level digital dharma, with its focus on discernment, advances into public awareness, the fourth-chakra-focused medium of television is struggling to remake itself. As discussed in the last chapter, naive optimism and unchecked consumerism no longer suffice for a new generation who were raised to question institutional honesty and who see themselves as media producers as well as consumers. Sensational "reality" programs and entertainment-driven "news magazines" strip away the happy facade of domestic family life, while the traditional showcase of socially committed documentaries, PBS, suffers severe budget cuts and heavy-handed political interference. Trust in the neutrality of commercial television news programs is at an all-time low. "Metainformation" shows (programs about programs) proliferate, while the fifth-chakra Internet has produced a whole new generation of savvy media critics.[69]

The multidimensional, interactive realm of the Internet and video games has forced TV and movies to become more complex. Traditional narrative programming relies on cheap emotional triggers aimed directly at fourth-chakra empathy receptors. The new prime-time successes rely less on emotionalism and more on social intelligence, strategic thinking, and community. According to journalist Steven Johnson, the new digital generation demands intelligent engagement: "Today's reality programming," he writes, "is reliably structured like a videogame: a series of competitive tests, growing more challenging over time."[70]

The "up-leveling" of television attempts to engage not only hearts and minds, but also social networks. Television programs are increasingly linked with Web sites where fans can analyze their favorite shows with the kind of scholarly devotion more often associated with the study of the Talmud, says Johnson.[71] Most shows (and their stars) have popular Web sites; many are decidedly unofficial. At least one new broadcast network (founded by former Vice President Al Gore and others) is experimenting with the P2P model: The cable channel Current shows viewers' videos (and even viewer-created advertisements), submitted by Internet, and allows the audience to vote for their favorites. Short "info-pods" display the most requested Google queries every half-hour.[72]

On the other hand, fourth-level, self-indulgent, and escapist "boomer" values can be found everywhere in cyberspace, from the almost infinite ways to shop, to a blogosphere flooded with millions of ego-centered opinions on everything from boyfriends to restaurant menus, to a video-sharing service catering to two-minute attention spans. This is the cyberspace where, as Frank Rich wrote in the *New York Times*, "Britney Spears Nude on Beach" had been viewed 1,041,776 times by YouTube's visitors. The count for all YouTube video clips tagged with "Iraq" was 22,783.[73]

The Net has taught us many new metaphors appropriate to fifth-level dharma. We have created in our "outer" nervous system what I believe is a technology of deep ecology, where overlapping processes and small networks, not individual isolated decisions, determine the outcome of our intentions. Packet-switching protocols are analogous to the path to knowledge, with its numerous detours and "routers" that challenge one's authenticity along the way. The invention of multidimensional, live, link-embedded hypertext is a perfect spiritual metaphor for Indra's Web, wherein all things are connected to every other thing, nothing is truly independent, nothing (and nobody) stands alone. In fifth-level awareness we are challenged to recognize that our information technologies reflect the multifaceted, interdynamic nature of creation. At the sixth level, the question is, "What is the reality behind this incredible web?" This is the work of the sixth chakra, and the focus of the next chapter.

LIVING IN FULL FIFTH-LEVEL TELECONSCIOUSNESS

In life as online, what you give and receive ideally reflect conscious choice. This manner of living requires honesty, selflessness, and presence. If the Web is a model of the Universe's infinite potential, every search, every page you visit, every link you follow becomes your chosen path and the opportunity to manifest your highest state of being.

As the neck is the junction between the brain and body, so is the fifth chakra the "nexus" between the compassion of the heart and the wisdom of the mind. The challenge is honest communications: Can you tell the truth—and confront lies—compassionately? Old defenses, guilt, self-righteousness, and manipulation no longer work in a world where everyone can see your inner light *and* your darkest shadow. In a world where every e-mail or text message is digitally stored somewhere, I find that I am constantly reminded that every word I speak is indeed given a life, that every one of my thoughts takes on an etheric form and joins all the other thoughts in mass consciousness.[74] In a world where vast reservoirs of pornography and violence are encoded on media servers that respect no boundaries and overcome most filtering software, none of us can avoid those uncomfortable conversations with our children (whether our offspring or the ones still within us) about the power of pain twisted to anger and about the lure of using fantasy and masturbation to meet our deepest hunger for connection.

Fifth-level digital dharma calls for communicating with what gestalt therapist Brad Blanton calls "radical honesty,"[75] showing your true Self to the world, dropping the mask of personality defense so that you can see the light in others. For we can only connect to the essential core of another—in person or in cyberspace— by greeting them from this true Self within. This level of connection requires that we call forth what Ambika Wauters calls the Communicator archetype and speak our truth to power. A person living from this archetype stands by his or her word and can be trusted with vital information:

> The Communicator speaks from its Higher Self and expresses its feelings and thoughts with alacrity and purpose. It neither gossips, criticizes nor curses and has a special regard for the spoken and written message.... This archetype knows that its spirit is diminished every time it lies, cheats or is grandiose.... It does not let people down with empty promises or false hopes.[76]

Meditation is one way to activate these higher Communicator energies. In a hyperstimulated media world, silence clears the mental "memory buffers," and the "roof-brain chatter" that passes for authentic Self. Mind clarification must precede mind expansion.[77]

These moments of silence are the inner firewalls against the waves of cultural spam that threaten to inundate us. From this place of deep quiet we can perceive the whole network: packets, routers, congestion, viruses, and all. Then we can, in Sri Aurobindo's words, "universalize ourselves till we are one with all being."[78]

By opening to "network consciousness" one can hold all of the data available to our physical—and spiritual—sense organs. But this new state of energetic interconnectedness requires courage. It means relinquishing one's distorted egocentric view of the universe. Just as computer networks evolved from central mainframes and dumb terminals through client/server models to today's distributed peer-to-peer intelligent networks, embracing fifth-level digital dharma requires that one move from a me-centered universe to a more ecological understanding. The challenge, of course, is to remain open to our multiple webs of connection while protecting ourselves from predators. Affiliating with trusted friends and supporting each other's work for planetary and personal healing creates the "small network" that can stabilize and hold our center as we move out to explore the light and shadow of our new expanded self.[79]

SUGGESTIONS FOR "INTERNET YOGA"

- Each time you go online, ask, "What is the truth here?" "Whose truth is it?" Ask yourself, "How do I decide what and whom to trust?"

- When you encounter a "questionable" site (perhaps dishonest or based in fear or hate), center yourself and send love to its creators. Visualize their true faces behind the aliases and Net names; see the Light in their hearts; hold them in love; then release your connection.

FIFTH-LEVEL TELECONSCIOUSNESS VISUALIZATIONS

Reassembling the Packets

First connect with your Higher Self; now set your intention to collect the fragmented "packets" of your life that have been lost across the net. Some may be those repressed and suppressed parts that are not so acceptable in "spiritual circles." Invite them home; bring them first into your belly, and then up into your heart. Despite their bad behavior, they may be some of your greatest teachers. Bring the power of the Light to your "Soul Router," your heart. Let it become bright white or golden or pink. Ask that the fragments be reassembled in the correct order. Envision a screen waiting to be filled with the deepest truth. What is the true message of your heart? It can be displayed in words, a picture, or movie.

Firewalls in the Field

First, connect with your Higher Self; now become aware of your energy field, especially around the throat chakra. Ask to see any obstacles preventing you from speaking only truth. What filters do you use? Do they need cleaning? Recalibrating? Are they effective or obstructive? Are they quiet or noisy? Imagine returning to a time when your filters became distorted. Who needs to be forgiven for hurting or lying to you? How can you unlearn mistrust and deception?

Visualize someone you need to address but to whom you find it difficult to communicate your true feelings. See that person on screen; ask the core of your heart to type the message you want to send. Make your words clear and truthful. Say it out loud. Be as assertive as necessary, without aggression. See your words traveling across the world's net, touching all the others in your universe, clearing out the cobwebs of falsehoods, aligning all of the waves radiating from every human's fifth chakra into a strong, clear, coherent symphony of *satya*—the truth of that which just simply *is*.

Planetary Healing

Visualize Indra's Net, the web around the planet; use universal love to cleanse the viruses, sending them to the Light. Picture that net being filled with the pure Light of your clear communications, awakening it to its true nature. Visualize your own web of trusted friends, and connect heart to heart. Finally, create a strong, effective "protection filter" for all your adventures in cyberspace.

SIXTH-LEVEL
DIGITAL DHARMA

SEEING DEEPER,
SEEING WIDER

The core personal metaphor of sixth-level digital dharma is "deep seeing," that is, moving from focusing on what's in front of us to expanding our vision to take in the big picture of reality. This level of awareness, often realized through intense spiritual practices (and sometimes via equally intense psychedelics or spontaneous breakthrough situations) is awareness apart from the thinking mind. It involves processing the data from the outer world in full consciousness that one is in fact data processing.

This book's first two chapters connected telegraphy, text messaging (SMS), radio-frequency identification (RFID), and telephony to the challenges of personal communications and body-centered awareness. The middle three chapters looked at how radio, television, and the Internet teach us about relationship to others. Now we explore the emerging technologies of digital media and pervasive "grid" computing—true second-tier technologies that model the advanced psychosocial developmental work of the transpersonal realm.

Sixth-level thinking is by its nature holographic, holding all levels of the greater information- and energy-filled "metauniverse" in awareness and appreciation; thus, it is free to see deeper, to tune across the whole range of consciousness.[1] This level of digital dharma is about learning to communicate beyond the surface forms, to connect soul to soul. In energy yoga, this communications transponder is centered at the "third eye," the organ of visual, psychic, and intuitive perception. Its element is light, and its task is to open our imagination to an expanded awareness that sees through what Sri Aurobindo calls "the eye of complete union."[2]

From this place, the old, habitual mindset no longer satisfies. All levels of reality, all ways of seeing the world, are open for fearless exploration: Experience is all there is. Cocreation and collaboration are the social organizing principles at this level. Out in the day-to-day world, one's dharma is to become a "systems seer," seeing and respecting every individual's and every culture's belief system, freely and compassionately interacting across all beliefs and psychological languages.[3] Sixth-level digital dharma requires one to widen one's reception channels, to take in more frequencies, to consider other "truths" than those one is most attached to. This evolution is the practice of turning from the limited data of the ego-self to something much bigger. On an inner spiritual level, Buddhism calls the sixth-level realm of perception *Dharmadhatu*, the realm of all dharmas, where all possible past, present, and future realities coexist; where what we call "darkness" and "light" are united once again. It is a state of peace where emptiness and the arising of form are in balance, where to see one object is to see all objects, or, in poet William Blake's words, "to see a world in a grain of sand, and a heaven in a wild flower."[4]

In this state of awareness, commonplace things radiate their essence. The eye is opened to the cosmic, but grounded in compassion. It decodes all incoming signals and discerns which ones to act upon, knowing all the time (as yoga philosophy tells us) that there is always more than one story to believe. In this state, the inner vision recognizes that all the stories of the manifest world, with its attributes, functions, and relationships, are but *maya*, fleeting illusions of concreteness in time and space that are essentially false.[5] Sixth-level awareness sees beyond the body into the cells and the DNA; it sees not only the individual frames of each "life story cartoon," but the "cels" that created the projector, screen, theatre, and audience as well!

The mystic's eye sees beyond superficial appearance and personal characteristics, beyond habitual concepts, to the true self in the other; to what the Hindus call *Advaita*, the true state of nonduality; to the underlying light of pure (*Brahman*) consciousness, which "modulates" all reality. It understands intuitively what Marshall McLuhan told us fifty-plus years ago: Pay attention to the underlying medium, and do not get hung up on each of the specific messages.[6] As the Sufi poet Jelaluddin Rumi wrote more than 750 years ago, we need to remember that

> When a strong wind blows,
> It rushes through windows
> And lifts carpets and levitates straw.
> A pond looks like rippled armour.
> Branches, leaves and trees dance.
> All these things look different,
> But in root and reality they're one:
> The wind.[7]

When the mind is prematurely opened to sixth-level awareness but not grounded in the lower centers, when the filtering systems of fifth-level dharma are not fully developed, the nervous system cannot handle the shock of seeing beyond the veil. For some, the result may be false insights and delusional "messages" from God. More often, we simply get lost in our own knotty ego projections, the mind's palace of mirrors.[8] At its worst, the sixth level becomes a place where nothing can be trusted, where, as in the nightmare worlds of *Blade Runner, Total Recall,* and *Minority Report* (all created by 1950s science-fiction writer Phillip K. Dick), "dreams are real, and reality turns out to be a dream."[9] I believe that our interconnected, packet-based Web technologies have indeed thrown us beyond the veil, whether we are prepared or not. Sixth-level digital dharma requires us to embrace the "all seeing," all-spectrum quality of the divine.[10] Our only other choice is to turn away into a deconstructed universe, where nothing seems to exist but cleverness and special effects.

The Infosphere's sixth-level technologies are megapixel cameras, camcorders, and photo cellphones; DVD players; and high-definition television (HDTV) receivers. All of these tools are based on the digital encoding and manipulation of what we think we see. They all openly rely on illusion, on the creation of digital sound and image files that trick the brain into creating more than what has actually been delivered to the retina and eardrum. Just as we routinely use digital editing software to adjust the "reality" of our digitized experience—to crop and zoom; choose a point of view; change colors, contrast, and brightness—our media challenge us to explore our point of view, to look wider and deeper, to focus on the once-hidden details of our visual field. Metaphorically, these media ask us to focus on the shadows, blurred lines, and comfortable concepts that have thus far defined our personal reality.[11]

Random-access technologies such as DVDs invite audiences to actively play with the unfolding of the traditional storyline. DVDs allow the viewer to experiment with temporal order by adding a second dimension to the linear flow of a story, perhaps by skipping forward or back, jumping to alternative shots, or watching the same story with a different soundtrack. No longer a passive receiver, one can interrupt, request more information, read the script, interview the performers, listen to the director's commentary, and try out different endings.[12]

High-definition television (HDTV) brings into our homes panoramic wide-screen images of incredible resolution and clarity. Its image signals contain double the scanning lines, ten times the pixels, and a viewing field one-third wider than the old analog TV screen. Viewers are freed from the restraint of the close-up and overt (fourth-level) emotional cuing. Information comes from the perimeter as well as the center of the picture. There is more to see, and the viewer is now responsible for deciding what parts of the screen to focus on. With the high-definition screen, the cinematic "two-shot"—two characters, two voices, two actions— is back, returning diversity and ambiguity to the TV image. Wide-angle shots reveal not just the batter on plate, but the entire field of action. Close-ups show every blemish.[13] New cameras under development promise an immersive 360-degree high-resolution "elective cinema" experience, allowing the viewer to focus on the hundreds of concurrent "inadvertent dramas" happening all around her.[14]

Along with the main digital video transmission in HDTV, a "datacast" subset of the signal can deliver Web content, multimedia e-mail, and even control signals to your home thermostat. Within the veritable sea of digital sound, text, and image data streams is a critical "PSIP" (program and system information protocol) code that deciphers them all and routes the picture to the screen, the data to the computer, and the Dolby™ audio to your surround-sound system. Without the correct decoding signal, all this data can be received, but not processed.

Today's cellular and cordless telephones, as well as many other digital radios used for secure communications, operate on similar sixth-level principles of "decoding." These devices use frequency-agile spread-spectrum transmitters, which, instead of sending a message in a narrow channel, "spread it out" and send it in pieces across a wide frequency range. The receiver follows the shift in frequencies by decoding a location signal sent in the transmission. Only a receiver synchronized to make the same frequency jumps can reassemble the bits in the correct order. Otherwise, all that is heard is noise.[15]

This frequency-hopping technique was coinvented by Hollywood actress Hedy Lamarr (figure 6.1) and composer George Antheil during World War II, to help direct American torpedoes and prevent them from getting jammed and diverted off target.

Figure 6.1. Hedy Lamarr

Their proposed arrangement used a synchronized mechanical switching system, similar to a player piano roll, to shift control frequencies faster than the enemy could follow. Each "note" marked on the piano roll corresponded to a frequency (figure 6.2). Synching the transmitter and receiver rolls meant that whenever a new "note" was "played," the radios would simultaneously switch frequencies. The line of communication was always open, though it seemed to switch quickly and erratically.

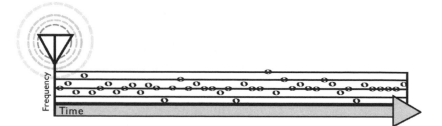

Figure 6.2. Spread-spectrum frequency distribution

On August 11, 1942, Lamar and Antheil were granted U.S. patent 2,292,387 for a "Secret Communications System." The concept was taken up by engineers in 1957 and became the basic tool for secure military communications—and for much of today's wireless digital traffic.[16]

The importance of having the correct signal to unravel the abundant "data stream of reality" is the underlying truth of sixth-level dharma wisdom. This need is reflected in our contemporary cultural fascination with codes—*The DaVinci Code*, *The Matrix*, genetic codes, security codes—and in the digital media tools of our age. The technologies of digital compression, those handy applications that reduce our music and video files to smaller and smaller sizes, all use hyperfast signal processors to convert "real world" analog images (or in the case of audio, the sound) into numeric computer codes. These codes are in turn reduced in complexity and sent on to control the manufacturing of an "acceptable proxy" of the original captured image. Digital "instruction-set" transmission is much more efficient and error-free than analog representation: It's like sending the recipe, not the cake. This ability to communicate the "recipe" is why language is more efficient than grunts and growls, why written alphabets are better than pictograms, and why DNA can perpetuate every living species with barely a flaw in billions of transmissions.[17]

Digital encoding and compression are not solely engineering strategies. These modes also govern how the brain processes what we "see." The visual world is so complex that storing even tiny fractions of the changing image would overwhelm even the vast storage system of the brain. Instead, the brain discards most of the information and relies on its own version of pattern encoding, converting analog images to a limited set of mathematical wave-pattern representations (called Fourier transforms) to tap memory and build its picture of the world.[18] The visual image we see, says Howard Bloom, "is the product of slicing, dicing, coding, compression, long-distance transmission, and neural guesswork:

Cells in the retina scrap 75 percent of the light which pours in through the lens of the eye . . . they fiddle with the contrast, tamper with the sense of space, and report not the location of what we're watching, but where the retinal cells calculate it soon *will* be . . . Adding insult to injury, the eye crushes the information it's already fuddled, compacting the landslide of data from 125 million neurons down to a code able to squeeze through a cable—the optic nerve—a mere 1 million neurons in size. On the way to the brain, the constricted stream stops briefly in the thalamus, where it is mixed, matched and modified with the flow of input from the ears, muscles, fingertips, and even sensors indicating the tilt and trajectory of the head, hands, legs, and torso.[19]

As evolutionary psychologist and meme expert Susan Blackmore tells us, when we look out a window, we may have the impression of a beautifully rich visual image, but in fact we're beholding only a compressed piece of the whole. "All our brains are holding is a little piece of the central image, a very rough sketch of the rest, and the ability to respond quickly to change and look again when necessary."[20] PBS technology guru Robert Cringely agrees:

So the retina makes an estimate of a visual scene or image based upon evolutionary knowledge of the statistical structure of natural scenes. The retina then estimates the likely error in that original estimate. Each of these functions is embodied in a specific segment of the retinal architecture. The retina then transmits to the rest of the brain what can be described as a real-time, 2-dimensional map of the likely error or uncertainty of the original estimate . . . What we "see" isn't the scene itself so much as an error map of the scene. We map the cliffs and potholes then paint the rest of the scene in our minds from stored image data.[21]

Science is showing us that we are prewired for recognizing certain objects (such as faces) and that what we "see" is based as much on past habits of seeing as it is on the new data coming into our eyes.

We do this all the time with text (see "Typoglycemia" box), and we do it all the time with images.

"Typoglycemia"

I cdnuolt blveiee taht I cluod aulacity uesdnatnrd waht I was rdanieg. The phaonmneal pweor of the hmuan mnid. Aoccdrnig to rscheearch at Cmabridge Uinervtisy it deosn't mttaer in waht oredr the ltteers in a wrod are. The olny iprmoatnt tihng is taht the frist and lsat ltteer be in the rghit pclae. The rset can be a taotl mses and you can sitll raed it wouthit a porbelm. Tihs is bcuseae the huamn mnid deos not raed ervey lteter by istlef, but the wrod as a wlohe. Amzanig, huh? Yaeh, and I awlyas thought sipeling was ipmorantt!

—Circulated on multiple blogs in April 2005.[22]

Basically, much of what we see is really fake! Or as Richard Grossinger chides us:

Ninety-nine percent of reality has nothing to do with vision, in fact nothing to do with anything, any of the thoughts running through our minds. Ninety-nine percent of the reason we want to live rather than die has nothing to do with what we tell ourselves makes us happy. Ninety-nine percent is simply here, with no perspective from which to view it, no surfaces by which to identify it, no language to reveal it to itself.[23]

The Infosphere's digitally compressed audio MP3s, video Web streams, DVDs, and HDTV all work on the same principles: analog-to-digital conversion, statistical compression, and inference. New audio and video data is compared to the data already received and decoded, and only the changes are passed on. Everything else is based on our "perceptual expectations" and stored "algorithms of importance." In fact, the experience of "reality" is always a half-second behind—that's the latency time of our visual consciousness, the time it takes for our inner decoder to grind away and produce its facsimile of truth.[24] Blackmore argues that our experience of "self" (in her terms, the "selfplex") is itself the result, not the cause, of our need to send and receive meme snippets of coded ideas.[25]

MPEG Video Compression Techniques

Video compression systems work by first narrowing the image in each frame down to its essentials—eliminating changes in color, motion, and brightness information that the brain cannot recognize or process fast enough to notice. Compression is accomplished by four basic techniques: pre-processing, temporal prediction, motion compensation, and quantification coding.

Pre-processing filters out non-essential visual information from the video signal. For example, color information is less important to the brain than grayscale data, which it uses to define boundaries between objects. So more color information is discarded than luminance data.

Temporal prediction takes advantage of the fact that most video frames are similar to those that precede and follow.

Motion compensation is accomplished by identifying the part of the frame that is moving, and with what direction and speed.

Quantification coding uses a mathematical algorithm to

reorganize the difference between frames into a series of numbers that can be more quickly transmitted. Whenever portions (blocks) of a frame differ, a code sequence is created that represents the difference. Where the value is close, a compromise number is sent for the entire block. Where entire blocks are repeated, only the first value is sent, followed by the "repeat this value X number of times" command.

MPEG 2 compression provides for up to three types of frames (figure 6.3) called "P," "B," and "I." The intra-frame, or "I" frame, serves as a reference for predicting subsequent frames. An "I" frame, which occurs on an average of one out of every ten to fifteen frames, only contains information presented within itself. "P" frames are predicted from information presented in the nearest pre-ceding "I" or "P" frame, while "B" frames are "bi-direc-tionally predicted" by averaging a forward and backward prediction.[26]

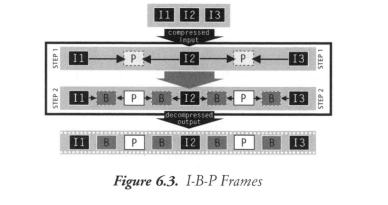

Figure 6.3. *I-B-P Frames*

Sixth-level digital dharma asks us to recognize that we are *always* processing codes of consensual reality and to pay attention to where we put our attention. Doing practices that open one to this stage of awareness is a form of "esoteric signal decompression" that allows one to look beneath surface identities to decode richer and subtler dimensions. Without preloaded (i.e., habitual) coding schemes, the fully aware brain takes in each new signal with fresh wonder as a sacred surprise; each sensory stimulus is decoded in the immediacy of the now, without reference to old memory patterns. At its best, unclouded sixth-level vision brings one closer to experiencing the unity of creation, seeing its underlying continuity, and hearing the hidden harmonies behind humanity's often painful apparent differences.

For the vast majority of us, full sixth-level seeing remains a distant goal. Opening to all incoming data can drive one to terror, and focusing too much on one slice of perception can lead to the "oh wow, man" stupor that is the butt of pot-smoker jokes. Without a strong grounding at the lower levels and good "truth filters" at the fifth chakra, the esoteric eye can be overwhelmed. When closed in self-defense, it refuses to accept conflicting information or complex memories and focuses instead on black or white answers. This is the challenge our digital technologies put before us. As Erik Davis observes, "the logic of [today's digital] technology has become invisible—literally *occult*. Without the code, you're mystified. And nobody has all the codes anymore."[27]

The light and the shadow of sixth-level communications dharma are reflected in our popular arts. The 1950s science-fiction stories of Phillip K. Dick are today's hottest Hollywood action-movie properties, while Neal Stephenson's historical novels about codes, viruses, and "the hacker grail" have made him, according to a review in the *New York Times*, "a cult figure among the digerati."[28] In the immensely popular thrillers of the *Matrix* series, the hacker's power lies in mastering the codes of consensual reality. The popular book *The Da Vinci Code*, with its clues and messages hidden in artwork, gravestones, and classical poetry, parallels the surreptitious appearance of "virtual products" and corporate logos in public places and in TV programs.[29] The 2004–2005 TV series *Joan of Arcadia* disguises God as "a stranger on the bus." On another show, TV detectives get help from a medium who hears crime victims from "the other side." The TV show *CSI* features crime-scene investigators who distill the truth from microscopic DNA crime-scene evidence. In many mosques, churches, and temples, fundamentalists offer simple solutions to today's complex problems by offering up their simple interpretations of esoteric "coded" verses. In the political domain, arguments over what "encodes" sexual identity have spilled over into battles over state Constitutional amendments.

When faced with the world's complexity, a closed sixth chakra refuses that complexity and vainly hangs on to the idea that "one magic code" will make sense of the world. In contrast, a "blown open" sixth no longer tries to ground the flow of information it receives into a coherent narrative; every new image becomes, in novelist Alan Lightman's words, "a disembodied nothingness," floating weightless in a sea of "digital emptiness."[30] For some, ungrounded media saturation has led to fascination with cults and magic. Many others have found themselves lost between physical and virtual realities, adrift in the video worlds of *Grand Theft: Auto* and *Mortal Kombat*.[31] These phenomenally successful (and addictive) video games combine high-definition video images, surround sound, and full interactivity with the experience of moving deeper and deeper into sixth-level-style "realities" that feature the sweet lure of sexuality and personal power. Given that seductive combination, it's no surprise that market forces have made the video-game industry into a $31-billion global business ($10 billion in the United States) that supplies games to more than 175 million players in the U.S. alone.[32]

Most of us, however, find ourselves between these two extremes, trying to make sense of our sixth-level media environment, trying to see more, to see wider, to see deeper in a world where everything is in the process of being digitized, where soon our entire culture will be delivered to our living rooms and pocket devices, our cars and computers, our eyes and ears, as strings of ones and zeros. Notwithstanding the popular image of compulsive teens hooked on violent video games (the *Grand Theft: Auto* series of games has sold more than 21 million copies since 2001), or the rise of "professional gamers" who play in public competitions for large cash prizes, the real video-game megahits are virtual sports leagues and online social simulation games such as *SimCity*. While the ranks of the sports leagues are filled with adult men, the simulation games are massively popular with both boys and girls, who can create entire worlds: agricultural villages, vast industrial megacities, high-tech edge cities, or small, pedestrian-friendly communities. The *Sim* series of games—which took the world-creating project down to the level of the neighborhood street—has sold three times as many copies as the *Grand Theft* franchise, generating over $1.6 billion in sales since its initial release in 2000.

A growing segment of the game market is devoted to positive social change: many games now address real-world problems, from Palestine to the former Yugoslavia. The second most popular downloaded simulation game of 2005 was *Food Force*. According to the United Nations World Food Program, "the game contains six different missions for children 8–13 years old, who are faced with a number of realistic challenges. In a race against time, they must feed thousands of people in the fictitious island of Sheylan; they pilot helicopters while looking out for hungry people; negotiate with armed rebels blocking a food convoy; and use food aid to help rebuild communities."[33]

Author Steven Johnson tells us these open-ended games work not just because they foster playing with possibilities, but also because they tap into the human spirit's sixth-level desire to see more. You want to build the building "not because it's there, but rather because it's not there, or not there *yet*."[34] Online multiplayer simulation games, played simultaneously by thousands, invite players to try out new roles and alter egos, to become parts of "communities of practice," and fully experience novel ways of thinking—and other realities—that print can only describe.

Virtual worlds are being created, populated, and socially activated by communities of users controlling their online "avatars." On the popular massive multiplayer online-simulation community *Second Life* (figure 6.4), one can buy virtual clothes or start a business or build a house. If you sign off and return a few days later, you may find that someone has built a house next door or dammed the river above your part of town. Real "off-line" companies such as

IBM and schools such as Harvard Law School have their own islands; nonprofit groups recruit members, and political-candidate avatars have already appeared.[35]

Young and old alike are attracted to the camaraderie and friendship of these online worlds and can even experience grief when their network of affiliation collapses. Natural-language interactive dramas are on the drawing boards, promising, in the words of one designer interviewed for the *Atlantic Monthly*, that "games will be as personal to you as your dreams, and as emotionally deep and meaningful to you as your dreams." For today's young people, games are an emerging art form, generating no less debate than motion pictures did nearly a century ago.[36]

Figure 6.4. *Hanging out in* Second Life

Our contemporary hunger for "seeing" has been reflected in the multiyear debate over repairing the Hubble Telescope and, closer to home, in the explosion of Internet Webcams—surveillance cameras, "nature cams," "traffic cams," and, for exhibitionists, "voyeur cams." Patrick DiJusto, a *New York Times* reporter, found more than 10,000 Web-linked cameras "showing everything from bedrooms and living rooms to coin-operated laundries and shoe stores to plasma reactors and mountain ranges."[37] But beyond seeing more is the challenge of seeing deeper. We are creating technologies that remind us not only to take in the wider view of life, but also to dig below, and up beyond, the surface pixels that seem to make up our day-to-day reality.

Long-zoom consciousness—reflected by our digital capability to "zoom out" from the scale of DNA through Google Earth's satellite maps to the enormity of the cosmos—is emerging as contemporary culture's defining way of seeing. It has created a new view of space as interconnected and multilayered that is as disruptive to our old ways of seeing as the earlier revolutions of Newton and Einstein.[38] "Deeper seeing" is the core metaphor of sixth-level digital dharma; it encapsulates the wisdom taught by contemporary philosophers and by the esoteric practices of ancient traditions. It is from this "big picture" place of compassion, beyond the world of form, that one can watch the consensual codes of the "causal realm" unfold and become "real" in the ever-forming Now. From this viewpoint, our world is not a *Matrix*-like evil dream, but a constantly redefined universal *Wikipedia*—the sum total of our belief systems. In a few years our analog television sets will go dark unless we upgrade them to receive the new digital transmissions. I believe that this technology shift in the Infosphere is also suggesting that it is now time for us to switch to a higher-definition way of seeing.

LIVING IN FULL SIXTH-LEVEL TELECONSCIOUSNESS

I have suggested that the Infosphere provides a set of metaphors that challenge us to see with the unfiltered eye, demonstrating in MPEG compression programs etched into silicon chips how we too create our consensual "stories" through patterns of prediction based on limited data. Our sixth-level dharma challenge is to see beyond preconceived appearances to the creative causes behind the veil of *maya*. We are asked to change our "spiritual operating system," to discard the embedded habitual "reference frames" that keep us from seeing with ever-fresh eyes and from fully experiencing the unfolding of the ever-present moment.[39]

Fifth-level digital technologies gave us a place to experiment with the "truth" by taking on different personalities, trying on different roles in the drama of life. Sixth-level awareness challenges us to step back and see the drama itself as a constructed event. Every time we put a CD or DVD into a playback device, we can remember that life itself is an encoded story; every time we manipulate the virtual reality of a video game or immersive digital experience, we can step back and ask how our own everyday reality is the product of similar manipulation and conjecture from limited knowledge. Like the blind men and the elephant, we are so certain of the truth of our small slice of the cosmos![40]

The brain already has in place the mechanisms for recognizing our "story codes." When stimulated by psychoactive substances, meditation, fasting, or prayer, it can release chemicals that suspend short-term memory and damp the background mental chatter, bringing one into the deep present moment where all creativity begins.[41] Some people choose drugs; for most of us, however, meditation is a less dangerous (and more socially acceptable) path to sixth-level seeing. From this place, one's intuition can tune into and decode the metaphors of the subconscious, the messages of dreams, and the universal truths of great art.[42] With practice, intuition can also "hear" the voices of one's personal spiritual guides and guide one back home to the seat of the Soul. All "magnetic" spiritual healing is based on sixth-level "energetic code repair." This healing draws on the Higher Self's intention and the power of the Universal Spirit to change psychological belief systems, heal wounds and pain held in the emotional energy field, release attachment to the story of past-life karma, or reset the codes controlling physical health.

Choosing to receive Spirit's blessing and to heal the pain of the past is a commitment to changing our perspective, to unlearning the compression scheme that decodes our experiences. In *The Sufi*

Book of Life, Neil Douglas-Klotz suggests that two of the ninety-nine Arabic names of God, *Al-Ghafur* (the Forgiver) and *Al-Afuw* (the Pardoner), are affirmations that have sixth-level power.[43] While their exoteric meaning for many worshippers is focused on (third-level) supplication to a judging power, the mystical, esoteric (sixth-level) invitation is to burn off old impressions (through the power of the Forgiver) and to blow away their ashes (through the power of the Pardoner), thereby clearing the dust from the surface of our heart. In chapter 4 I discussed *Al-Tawwâb*, the Beckoner of our Return, and its affirmation, *Ya-Tawwâb*. It has many meanings: to repent and to return to an all-forgiving Spirit; to "turn away" from the old, stuck beliefs; to forgive others and oneself; to, at the sixth-level of dharma, replace an old decoding scheme with a better one; to overwrite the stories of our wounding and our wounding of others. I meditate on these names as a reminder to "cleanse the buffer," to release the cleverness of the ego. Their goal is to facilitate a return to one's true nature, one's "original face," the uncluttered state of boundless mind "before it became conditioned, socialized, prejudiced, terrified."[44]

Meditation is, in effect, a process of observing the instruction codes of reality without processing them into thoughts, emotions, and suffering. We can choose whether to engage or to just observe the flow. We have the power to decide whether to identify with the stories of life experience or to be the silent observer of the codes. Our gullible consciousness responds to any software we put into it. A discerning awareness of our "programming" can take us out of our self-imposed prison of limitation. In the Vedic story we are introduced to two birds of the same name, "beautiful of wing, friends and comrades," clinging to a common tree. "One eats the sweet fruit, the other regards him and eats not."[45]

Sixth-level dharma is about deciding whether we want to identify with ego and its attachment to the fruits of externally modulated local reality, that is, the worldly dichotomies of pleasure and pain, success and failure, good and evil, or whether we want to move to the place of the silent observer, of full decompressed awareness, watching, as if on a video monitor, the multiple levels of reality unfold before our eyes. By using our big-picture zoom, we can practice expanding our field of awareness until all subjective understanding gives way to the universal Source, the quiet center where the underlying spirit of the universe is all there is. From this stance of loving observation, one can become, in Sri Aurobindo's words, more than "a laborer in a thought factory, but a receiver of knowledge from all the hundred realms of being."[46]

Vietnamese monk and master teacher Thich Nhat Hanh writes of sixth-level vision when he invites the reader to look deeper at the paper of the book in front of her. Behind the paper stand the tree; the logger; the light, water, and soil. "As thin as this sheet of paper is, it contains everything in the universe in it." Within the rose is the compost, within the compost, tomorrow's rose.[47] With access to all potential codes, one is free to choose a more loving and less fear-based life story from the library of Creation, repair one's karma, and, by following one's deepest aspirations, jump to a higher track of true service. One can make the idealistic themes of *Second Life* the fuel for transforming *this life.*[48]

From this big-seeing place it is easy to imagine unselfishly observing the shadowy programs of human suffering (without attachment to either outcome or being special in any way) and then taking them in and replacing them with a newly encoded "lighter" version for all of humanity.[49] What that ultimate "life track" might look like is the subject of the next chapter.

Installing Love Spiritual Support

Customer Service Rep: Yes. How can I help you?

Customer: Well, after much consideration, I've decided to install Love. Can you guide me through the process?

Rep: Yes. I can help you. Are you ready to proceed?

Customer: I can do that. I'm not very technical, but I think I am ready to install now. What do I do first?

Rep: The first step is to open your HEART. Have you located your HEART, ma'am?

Customer: Yes I have, but there are several programs running right now. Is it okay to install while they are running?

Rep: What programs are running, ma'am?

Customer: Let me see, I have PASTHURT.EXE, LOW-ESTEEM.EXE, GRUDGE.EXE, and RESENTMENT. COM running right now.

Rep: No problem. LOVE will automatically erase PAST HURT.EXE from your current operating system. It may remain in your permanent memory, but it will no longer disrupt other programs. LOVE will eventually overwrite LOWESTEEM.EXE with a module of its own called HIGHESTEEM.EXE. However, you have to completely turn off GRUDGE.EXE and RESENTMENT.COM. Those programs prevent LOVE from being properly installed. Can you turn those off, ma'am?

Customer: I don't know how to turn them off. Can you tell me how?

Rep: My pleasure. Go to your Start menu and invoke FORGIVENESS.EXE. Do this as many times as necessary until GRUDGE.EXE and RESENTMENT.COM have been completely erased.

Customer: Okay, I'm done. LOVE has started installing itself automatically. Is that normal?

Rep: Yes it is. You should receive a message that says it will reinstall for the life of your HEART. Do you see that message?

Customer: Yes I do. Is it completely installed?

Rep: Yes, but remember that you have only the base program. You need to begin connecting to other HEARTS in order to get the upgrades.

Customer: Oops . . . I have an error message already. What should I do?

Rep: What does the message say?

Customer: It says, "ERROR 412—PROGRAM NOT RUN ON INTERNAL COMPONENTS." What does that mean?

Rep: Don't worry ma'am, that's a common problem. It means that the LOVE program is set up to run on external HEARTS but has not yet been run on your HEART. It is one of those complicated programming things, but in non-technical terms it means you have to "LOVE" your own machine before it can "LOVE" others.

Customer: So what should I do?

Rep: Can you find the directory called "SELF-ACCEP-TANCE"?

Customer: Yes, I have it.

Rep: Excellent, you are getting good at this.

Customer: Thank you.

Rep: You're welcome. Click on the following files and then copy them to the "MYHEART" directory: FOR-GIVESELF.DOC, SELFESTEEM.TXT, REALIZE-WORTH.TXT, and GOODNESS.DOC. The system will overwrite any conflicting files and begin patching any faulty programming. Also, you need to delete SELF-CRITICIZE.EXE from all directories, and then empty your recycle bin afterwards to make sure it is completely gone and never comes back.

Customer: Got it. Hey! My HEART is filling up with

really neat files. SMILE.MPG is playing on my monitor right now and it shows that WARMTH.COM, PEACE. EXE, and CONTENTMENT.COM are copying themselves all over my HEART!

Rep: Then LOVE is installed and running. You should be able to handle it from here. One more thing before I go . . .

Customer: Yes?

Rep: LOVE is freeware. Be sure to give it and its various modules to everybody you meet. They will in turn share it with other people and they will return some really neat modules back to you.

Customer: I will.

—Source unknown[50]

SIXTH-LEVEL TELECONSCIOUSNESS VISUALIZATION

Recoding Old Beliefs

NOTE: Because this work involves more esoteric energies than the meditations for the lower chakras, it may not be appropriate for all people. Do NOT force this meditation. If you have a personal teacher or guide, do discuss it with him or her.

Sit in a comfortable chair. Relax. . . . Follow your breath to any place of tension. Release it. Let go of any thoughts. Ask your Higher Self to support you in this sixth-chakra clearing meditation. Feel your feet fully grounded; use your breath to imagine roots growing out of the base of your feet down to the center of the earth. Feel a safe curtain of Light rise from the earth and surround and permeate your energy field. Thank your Higher Self (and your name for the Divine) for this protection. . . . Set the intention of opening the third eye center at whatever level is safe for you.

Imagine a small network grid connecting your third eye (at the center of the forehead) to the pineal gland at the center of your brain, to the heart center, and to the physical visual cortex area in the brain. (You don't have to actually *know* where this is; it's the intention that counts.) Imagine light traversing this network. Slowly ask to "see" one of the patterns of your life that keeps you from fully living your potential. A person or a scene of some past or future event may appear in your expanded vision.

Ask to "see" the underlying pattern (the encoded belief system) that brought this challenge into your life. Gently ask to "zoom out" to a wider view. Using your fifth-level skills, ask to see the network patterns and "hooks" at play; maybe you've already projected the future outcome of some aspect of your life based on old ways of thinking. Use your skills from earlier visualizations to bring Light and forgiveness from your heart and from the Divine to anyone that helped create these patterns. Once one image is cleared, ask to zoom out to a wide view, releasing and forgiving at each step.

If you are comfortable with the idea of a Higher Being, ask the Being to help you rest in the peace of the "big picture." Try looking at the whole system as just a pattern being unwound, revealing the pure goodness behind the structures you have held as true. Turn your true face to the face of a loving God.

If you are uncomfortable with a deity, then consider the Buddhist mantra of the long zoom, the Heart Calming Mantra from the Heart Sutra: "*Gate, Gate, Paragate, Parasamgate, Bodhi Svaha*" (gone, gone, gone beyond, gone beyond the beyond into full enlightenment, so be it). Or you may consider the Vedanta yoga phrase "*neti-neti*" (not this, nor this). This latter mantra reminds one that we are truly not any of the coded stories that seem so important at the moment.[51]

When you are ready, reverse the zoom and slowly drop down to the cellular dimension. Visualize your core program being held in a CD-ROM running a few feet above your crown. Ask the Light to defragment this code; imagine negative belief-system subroutines being replaced with more positive operating instructions. Imagine a golden light rewriting the code of your life to its most positive outcome! Feel yourself turning to a new perspective. Thank Spirit. Gently bring your awareness from your energy field back to the Heart, then out to your skin and to your feet. Set an intention to manifest your new future! Open your eyes.

* * * * *

After doing this meditation a few times, you can set your intention to recode the communal patterns held in mass consciousness. Start first by changing the codes of fear holding your immediate friends and family, then your community, then your country, and then the world. At each level, see what needs to be changed and imagine it happening.

SEVENTH-LEVEL
DIGITAL DHARMA

TELECONSCIOUSNESS—THE UNITY
OF SELF AND THE COSMOS

Seventh-level communications takes us directly into the realm of the Divine, into "nonlocal" awareness that extends from the individual to the vast archetypal database of content that is "quantum mind." In personal transformational terms, this is the rarified place sought by all mystics: Unity—the simultaneous experiencing of the knower and the known, the divine expression of lover and the beloved.[1] Its literal, down-to-earth reflection in the social-political "values sphere" is Gaia consciousness: seeing the world as "a dynamic organism comprised of living systems that mesh and blend."[2] Out in the Infosphere, we call it "pervasive computing."

In the domain of the chakras, it is the transponder at the crown of the head—often represented by artists as the halo or aura of golden light around the world's great saints and masters—that modulates our link to the Divine. The archetypical holder of this energy is the Wise One, the Elder, the *Bodhisattva* or Saint, the mystical teacher that simultaneously holds the divine and the mundane, the universal and the individual, in one all-embracing loving consciousness. When we communicate from this center, we feel united with the omnipresent, indivisible transcendent unity field that is the true reality behind our world of personality, space, and time. This field, "known by many names," as Anodea Judith writes, "is the Tao, Brahma, Divine Mind, Allah, God, Universal Spirit, endless void, or the Power of Now that can only be entered through expanded consciousness."[3]

When seventh-level communications is severely blocked, a crisis of faith may occur; one may experience bouts of deep depression and chronic exhaustion. On the other hand, when this center is rapidly and prematurely opened, the resulting illumination may be overwhelming. Some find themselves vulnerable to terrorizing visions; others may want to leave the body behind for the "rapture" or a trip on the next flying saucer. In global terms, the fascination with communication from the "other side"—the "extraterrestrials, spirits, angels, ancestors, ascended avatars, Christ and Babaji in multiple forms and guises," as Richard Grossinger calls them—reflects the unfiltered leakage into the crown center of the Infosphere.[4] But when anchored by the heart and grounded to the earth, the crown center can safely connect one to the infinite shared database of all of human history, to the possibilities of spiritual transformation and energetic healing.[5]

In healthy seventh-level consciousness, one is aware of individuality but also has full knowledge of being part of a gigantic, joyous whole. Here, all boundaries are dissolved, and all is possible. One is at once all these things: a node on the network, and the entire web itself; the coding algorithms, and all of the world's decoders; a data packet traveling over a specific radio channel, and the entire spread-spectrum symphony of interference patterns, overlaps, and interactions between frequencies shared by everyone who has ever lived. At this stage of evolution, Sri Aurobindo tells us, awareness is free to "ascend the whole range of vibration of consciousness, from atom to Spirit . . . it remembers itself totally."[6]

While the high-definition, deep-seeing awareness of the sixth chakra allows the yogi to connect "everything within a single beam," its beam still ends in a single point of view. Seventh-level digital dharma, however, involves simultaneously seeing the point of view of each separate thing. It holds in its vision, not a single image, but the myriad of all points.[7] It can tune to—and compassionately understand—all sixth-level (spread-spectrum) frequencies of experience. It hears the sound that remains eternally unchanged in the midst of life's vast vibratory symphony.[8]

The reflection of this "always on, always connected" relationship with the infinite is found in the Infosphere at the convergence of a number of fifth- and sixth-level technologies: "grid," or distributed, information processing; nanotechnology and miniaturization; peer-to-peer communications; universal wireless connections; and GPS-based location awareness. These are the driving forces behind what is now being called pervasive computing, a set of technologies that will enliven the space we move through by permeating it with myriad ubiquitous, networked, mobile, reactive, and self-referencing miniature computational devices. The true impact of electricity had to wait until it literally "withdrew into the woodwork;" so too with the potentials of seventh-level communications and computing.[9]

Distributed processing technology allows for both software and computing processors to reside out on the network "grid" and be called forth only when needed. Extremely large scale computing projects can be shared across millions of smaller processors worldwide: Each processor "donates" its spare computing cycles to the functioning of the whole by running a small "seed program" in the background, as the user runs his or her regular applications. "The main idea," explains Jim Banister in *Word of Mouse*, "is to move data and computation off the desktop and fragment and distribute them throughout . . . a network smart enough to protect, distribute, and parse that data." He uses a core seventh-level metaphor when he describes grid computing as taking a piece of consciousness and putting it into the universal field:

> It would be as if you were able to take a math problem occupying your brain, or a large chunk of your childhood memories, and

break them down into individually unrecognizable fragments in order to distribute them throughout the brains of thousands or millions of your fellow humans, who might be better suited to handle that math problem, or who might have unused memory capacity.[10]

Grid computing networks are already tackling projects such as modeling of new cancer-fighting drugs, solving health challenges in Africa, tracking the smallest quantum interactions, and mapping the universe. In the last project, multiple smaller telescopes are being networked together across the university-based Internet2, making possible new forms of collaborative instrumentation and collaborative research. From an esoteric point of view, it is not surprising that one of the first (and still running) grid computing projects is focused outward to the vast universe—specifically, to the search for extraterrestrial intelligence (SETI). Operating since May 1999, SETI@home involves over two million users, each of whom analyzes a tiny portion of radio telescope data every night on their home PCs to detect signals from possible extraterrestrial civilizations. As of the end of 2006, the SETI project participants had cumulatively logged 2.7 million years of computing time.[11]

In a more popular setting, the major Internet portals and search engines such as Google and Yahoo distribute their computing resources across dozens of fiber-optic-linked data centers around the world. New network applications such as Jinni (Java INference Engine and Networked Interactor) and Ajax (Asynchronous Java-Script and XML) speed up Web applications by summoning snippets of data from across the network as needed instead of requesting the entire program from a central server. If the Ajax engine needs something from the server in order to respond to user input, it makes its request asynchronously "behind the scenes," while the user continues to interact with the program on her screen. Instead of massive proprietary files designed to run on single machines, these new Lego-like modular programs model seventh-level abundance. They are "open source"—freely available to all—and designed to be delivered as needed.[12]

In addition to shared processing cycles and Web applications, the Infosphere's abundance of text, music, video, spoken word, and other forms of artistic creation continues its migration to the Grid. That migration may eventually include every book written, every recording, every Web page, every film and television program—the collected works of humankind. New business models based on the "long tail" (the name Chris Anderson, a senior editor at *Wired*, has bestowed on publishers' neglected, nonbestseller backlists) have emerged to meet each person's idiosyncratic tastes.[13]

Peer-based, distributed file-sharing programs such as Bittorent are replacing many of the old centrally organized (and centrally stored) content services that profited from the illegal traffic in copyrighted files. These programs, which allow portions of the more-requested files to be parsed out and stored on the hard drives of hundreds of users, are seriously threatening the business models of those selling physical media. Several public television and radio stations have placed portions of their archives on the Web and encouraged users to share them under an intellectual "creative archive license." This footage can be viewed, downloaded, edited, and mixed, so long as it is for noncommercial personal use. In the United Kingdom, the BBC has gone even further, putting significant amounts of content online and encouraging its viewers to send in their videos of local news events and their creative remixes of the posted content. Google has begun the process of digitally scanning the collections of five major research libraries (including the New York Public Library and the University of Michigan and Stanford University libraries), making public-domain works, and eventually copyrighted texts, available to billions of readers worldwide.[14]

In this vision of the Grid, we simply ask for what we need, trusting our interconnected servers to hold, and our ever more powerful search engines to find, the best of this overflowing abundance. Today's Web-savvy generation trusts the Net to provide all that it seeks. They trust it to share its collective intelligence—the new and the old; the collages and mash-ups; the meshes, mixes, and remixes of popular culture; the music, photos, stories, journals, and interactive games—with their computers, MP3 players, digital television recorders, and cellphones.[15] The act of listening to radio or viewing video is being transformed from passively receiving (at third and fourth level) someone else's choices, to an active process of selecting programs from repositories around the world. By using RSS (really simple syndication), one can set one's Web browser to scan the Internet for announcements of only the audio podcasts one really desires and order them delivered while one sleeps. Soon, the same will be true for television programs; many of us already let the digital video recorder or TiVo find tonight's viewing from the hundreds of channels on cable or satellite.[16]

> Information Age thinking says, "Control the creation and distribution of information and you dominate markets." The Participation Age is the antithesis of that. It's all about access. That access allows for value to be created through networked human beings who share, interact, and solve problems. Because of participation, meaningful content, connections, and relationships are created like never before. In the Participation Age, there are no arbitrary distinctions between passengers and crew, actors and audience. Be one, be both, be everything in between.
>
> —Scott McNealy, Founder, Sun Microsystems, 2006[17]

Our computing devices are also getting smaller and smaller, and ever more specialized. Mirroring our first chakra, they will each have their own IP address and ability to "call out" their status. However, unlike simple RFID chips, they won't just send out one-way *Hineini* signals, but, being equipped with their own microprocessors, they will engage in dialog with every other nearby transmitter via wireless data connections.[18] Jerry Kang and Dana Cuff, at UCLA's Institute for Pervasive Computing and Society, describe this as the emergence of "PerC"—pervasive computing—which we will recognize "when the Internet gets ubiquitous, embedded, and animated."

Ubiquitous access to the Internet through mobile, wireless communications devices is just around the corner. . . . More important and less understood, the Internet will soon invade real space as networked computing elements become *embedded* into physical objects and environments. Through this implantation, physical objects and environments will gain digital qualities, such as computer addressibility through unique identification codes. They can also be endowed with new powers by implanting computing elements that are *animated*—they can not only sense their surroundings but also respond to them directly.[19]

PerC will extend cyberspace to the "real" space of our houses and shopping malls, to our appliances, clothing, and body parts. Eventually, home, office, and school devices will be networked; public spaces will be awash in unseen radio signals traveling between tiny RFID chips, smart appliances, cellphones, and GPS satellite receivers (figure 7.1). Internet access will be available

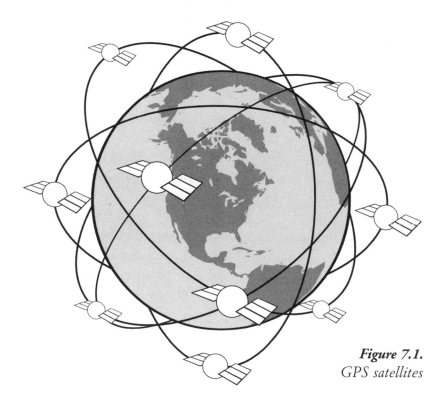

Figure 7.1.
GPS satellites

everywhere: in the air, in our kitchens and cars, in our sunglasses, in our clothing, and eventually (through the dispersal of smart nanosensors) inside our bodies. Instead of visiting the doctor's office for follow-up tests, your organs may soon call in their condition via Wi-Fi. As technology columnist Thomas Barnett quipped, "take two of these tonight and the doctor calls you in the morning!"[20]

Fifth-level digital dharma asks us to confront the vulnerability that comes with network interdependence: One is part of the Grid, but always a bit susceptible in an environment beyond one's control. At the seventh level, we are asked to live as if we are connected in all dimensions: horizontally to our families and our communities, and vertically to our common earth at one pole and our spiritual vision at the other. Michel Bauwens defines the new cooperative P2P network ethic as one where intelligence "is located not at any center, but everywhere, at the periphery of the system." A true P2P system, he explains, starts from the premise that "it doesn't know where the needed resource will be located"; rather, it assumes that "everybody" can cooperate and doesn't determine in advance who can participate. In this practice, one's "wisdom reputation" determines one's power; false data is subject to community scrutiny and correction; and the sharing of knowledge, not the hording of it, gains one respect.[21]

Out at the seventh level of the Infosphere, all devices know where they are, monitor their internal processes, go out on the Web for information, and routinely talk to each other. In this world, office machines call in service technicians before their owners are aware of any problems. Tiny sensors monitor soil and water conditions, alerting farmers when to irrigate and harvest. Similar devices embedded in bridges send wind, wave, and traffic data to the highway department.[22] Prototype Coke machines already adjust their prices depending on supply and the current weather and traffic conditions; they even call nearby delivery drivers when they need restocking.

On the domestic front, air conditioners and furnaces are being equipped to monitor weather forecasts and fuel costs and respond appropriately. Even our umbrellas and toasters can become intelligent network nodes: One student has designed a toaster that monitors the weather and "burns" a cloud, sun, or raindrop into the user's morning toast. And another company offers an umbrella with light-emitting diodes (LEDs) in the handle that flash faster with each uptick in the probability of rain.[23] Our microwave ovens will have an Internet link so that they can download recipes on demand. We'll be able to call the refrigerator to ask what's in it when we're at the store. Better yet, it will send us an e-mail telling us that the milk is going bad, or that we are low on orange juice.[24]

What's for Dinner? Just Call Your Refrigerator

You are at the office and decide to invite friends over for dinner that night. What's for dinner? Just pick up the phone and call home. Your kitchen can give you a heads up on what foods you have in the refrigerator and pantry, suggest menus that use some of those foods, and once you've selected the menu, it will supply a grocery list for other items you need to pick up. Use the same call to leave a message for your spouse to put some wine in the refrigerator to chill. Sound impossible?

—General Electric press release [25]

Beyond the web of communicating appliances is the seventh-level vision of an interconnected creative culture, where each person produces and shares his or her personal media across formats and across playback devices. And beyond this cultural vision is this spiritual teaching: We can create a world where all beings are simultaneously aware of their common Source (the universal intelligence of the Grid) and their power to download all the divine love and light their field can handle, all the guidance they need to create their individual life mission. Pervasive computing reminds us that seventh-chakra communication is not about sending "Here I Am" broadcasts and passively waiting for an acknowledgment. It is, in Sufi terms, sending out a call for the Beloved and having it answered tenfold.[26] In Matthew Fox's words, it is about true full-duplex communications across space and across time, past, present, and future:

> The seventh chakra is like a *beacon* or searchlight that extends into the heavens and into the past (our ancestors) and the future (our descendants) to make community happen. . . . The seventh chakra puts forth the light aroused in our being and searches for the light, *doxa*, glory, or wisdom in others. Indeed, it is light meeting light.[27]

Seventh-level dharma is about deciding to fully connect with every other being, and simultaneously with something greater than oneself. It means extending our sixth-level "long view" perspective of physical reality to something that crosses space and time, body and spirit. We are conscious of our own programs, but we also hold space for the greater field that connects us all. We understand that evil comes from the false identification with separateness. We live in the small slice of the universal hologram that is our individual life story and, at the same time, in the great field in which that hologram is embedded. The self, which first stepped into individuation as its first-stage dharma, is now strong enough to join the universal Self in its project of evolution, assisting God in discovering itself through each of us—God's countless, inimitable selves.[28]

Our work, according to Sri Aurobindo, is to bring back from the boundless realms of Light a new way of knowing—an illuminated awareness that lives simultaneously in the world of physical manifestation and in the mind of God. We are to add our individual ripple to the "sea of all that is and will be."[29]

In a world where every data device is intelligent, we must consciously choose to live this higher vision of the Infosphere. Left to the forces of the marketplace, seventh-level technologies can easily lead to a beehive-like world devoid of quiet personal space, a world where global corporations extend their control to the most remote corners of the planet; where the smallest personal action is tracked in giant marketing and "homeland security" databases; where physical nature and human love are replaced by computer simulations. In this impoverished world, "escape" is sold to us in the form of copy-protected, temporary-use-licensed, Hollywood-provided media experiences.[30] This dystopia—with endless distractions that keep the masses moving along, without ever being moved—would leave us, warns Buddhist scholar Peter Hershock, with an "unbroken forgetfulness of even the possibility of enlightenment."[31]

As with earlier advances in telecommunications, there is much to fear in unrestricted, ego- and capital-driven implementations of seventh-level technologies. We see it in the doomsday scenarios that proliferated around "Y2K" and in the belief by some that product barcodes are "marks of the Beast." But like all human creation, the Infosphere also holds a more positive vision of expanded consciousness: PerC mimics in silicon and radio waves a world where we are simultaneously witness, creator, and creation. In this world we effortlessly download from the "divine treasury" the entire wisdom of the quantum universe, along with the knowledge of how to use it; there, we know that the spiritual and the mundane are not so far apart.[32] In this state, as long as people haven't been seduced by the personal high of "dispersing into a luminous no-man's-land," in Satprem's words, they can use their own newly expanded consciousness "as a material link between the very top and the very bottom" of the spiritual ladder.[33]

> If in premodernity we thought, we are parts of a whole that is one and above us, and in modernity we thought we are separate and unified individuals, a world onto ourselves, and in postmodernity saw ourselves fragmenting, and pretty much lamented this, then this is the mash-up

> era. We now know that all this [sic] fragments can be reconstructed with the zillions of fragments of the others, into zillions of commonalities, into temporary wholes that are so many new creative projects, but all united in a ever-moving Commons that is open to all of us.
>
> —Michel Bauwens, "The Great Cosmic Mash-Up" [34]

The contemporary "field awareness" vision is not a return to premodern tribal consciousness but a move into a dynamic, networked dance of creative relationships in which numerous individuals join in playful and temporary combinations. The Grid has made possible entirely new seventh-level social relationships by "mashing up" programs and data from multiple sources and locations. A classic example reported in the *New York Times* was Paul Rademacher's integration of Google maps with the apartment listings on the craigslist sites for different cities. Similar geospatial mash-ups allow one to map local jobs, wireless hotspots, java joints, or, on a more serious note, registered sex offenders. Once the global library is online, every location on the planet could "know" everything that was ever written (or filmed or sung) about it.

As discussed in chapter 1, the addition of GPS chips to cellphones opens up all kinds of first-level *Hineini* security possibilities—and dark surveillance threats. At the seventh level, adding location awareness to our communications devices makes possible new ways of bringing the vast universe of Web resources down to the individual person at a unique time and place. One person's phone can point her to Mecca and help search the Web for a nearby mosque, while another's finds a particular type of restaurant and tells him how to get there. Soon, if you call a friend, you'll get block-by-block directions to her house; better yet, the phone will alert you if your friend happens to be sitting in a coffee shop nearby.

Several media artists are already bringing core seventh-level concepts into concrete reality. Some are experimenting with humorous ways that communications devices can cooperatively affect community space. One example is the Chaos Computer Club, a community of German hackers with a penchant for public art. They transformed a building in Berlin into a giant computer screen by making offices on the top eight floors light up like individual pixels. A computer controlled the lights in each room to produce a matrix of 18x8 pixels based on received SMS messages. *Blinkenlights*, as the installation was called, allowed people to send in messages, post animations (figure 7.2), and play Pong.[35] A few months earlier, computer science students at Brown University turned one side of the 14-story Sciences Library into a grid on which students could play online Tetris.[36] In Greenwich, England, in an event called Sky Ear (September 15, 2004) a cloud of helium balloons and cellphones was launched into the sky. Users could listen to the sky's electromagnetic sounds, and by "calling the cloud" they could also modify its environment and cause variations in brightness and color.[37] Some artists have used signals from the human body (such as dancers' movements and singers' voices) to shape shared environments, while others are using clothing itself as a communications display.[38]

Figure 7.2. Blinkenlights, *Berlin*

Beyond these playful uses of signaling technologies, I see the expression in the cultural sphere of a quality of awe and wonder at how consciousness networks itself: each node of individuality brings forth a unique story (karma) by its own actions and simultaneously creates new stories by its relation to every other being. To me, these artists are using the tools of seventh-level telecommunications to show us in chips and wireless nodes a concrete expression of what Sri Aurobindo called the next stage of human development: "infinite consciousness throwing up forms of self-expression, but aware always of its unbound infinity and universality."[39]

An early expression of beauty created through the act of networking was *Umbrella.net* (2004), in which ten participants carried Bluetooth-equipped umbrellas with accompanying PDAs running networking software. The umbrellas were illuminated by LEDs that pulsed red when the PDA was searching for others, pulsed blue when the PDAs were connected, and flashed when the participants were sending (or relaying) text messages between themselves. The artists take these "intelligent umbrellas" to cities around the world, allowing, in their words, "the haphazard and unpredictable patterns of weather and crowd formation" to create "a spontaneous network for sharing localized information among connected nodes." The colors of the devices, in turn, establish a visual footprint for all to see.[40]

Seventh-level dharma is about deciding to connect with every other being and simultaneously participate in the field of connection that thereby results. It means extending our perspective of physical reality (activated in sixth-level consciousness) to something that crosses space and time, body and spirit. It means staying conscious of one's operating programs, and, like the latest upgradeable nanochips, changing our codes to accommodate our true work.[41]

Like the wireless relay points on the "self-healing mesh networks" now covering our cities with ubiquitous Wi-Fi connectivity, each of us is called to pass on as many divine energetic messages as we can. And the message is always about love! We must become what Rumi calls a flute of God, a flute having one end in heaven and the other in our hearts. Our breath is the current that flows between the worlds: out to our partners on the network, and then back to

Source. Our true purpose is *tikkun olam* (repairing the net), assisting the Divine Self in discovering itself through each of us.[42]

LIVING IN FULL SEVENTH-LEVEL TELECONSCIOUSNESS

From "PerC" to "smart dust," the Infosphere is already modeling the not-yet-attained paradigm shift awaiting human consciousness. Seventh-level technologies show how people can be more than individual transmitters: We are part of a joyously noisy communicating system, and we must transcend the illusion of separateness to fulfill our destiny of planetary cocreation. When opened, the seventh chakra informs the first chakra that we are indeed never lost, and the first chakra can then respond by grounding this infusion of Spirit into the blood, bones, and skin of the physical body.

In seventh-level teleconsciousness, we are not only the *I* and the *Thou*, but also the network connecting them. As with the interactive art installations described above, the very act of communicating creates wonder. Not unlike the flashing LEDs in *Umbrella.net*, we can choose to remain conscious of our role as God's nervous system, responsible for creating the universe each time we see the other as a reflection of the Divine. Or we can send out negative thoughts that in the end, once on the network, rebound back to us multiplied in negativity and in power.[43]

Seventh-level communications is by its very nature mystical. In terms of our dharma lesson, one can be fully in the body, sending and receiving signals to other beings, and one can also be a vessel empty of ego, waiting to be of service to the Divine, waiting for new bits of cosmic code. Like smart RFID chips, we receive information from the Grid and radiate out our own individual bits of data; we absorb Spirit with our breath and breathe out this light through our own filters. Hazrat Inayat Khan, speaking almost a century ago, likened us to electric lamps all plugged into the same power source but each covered with a differently tinted globe, "and all these lights seen in many globes are called souls."[44]

Bringing these seventh-level communications models into our inner spiritual domain is the challenge ahead of us. For, with those models in place, we can become mystics of the Infosphere. Grounded, with strong centers and compassionate hearts, we will be ready to take the next step in our evolution: discovering that all we sought has been here all along. As we open to seventh-chakra energies, we will discover our ability to decode any message ever sent into the Infosphere; we will be free to acknowledge the *Hineini* call of every form of matter. Stepping back from the myth of separate transmitters, we will recapture the "flow" of creativity and communion: We will see worlds coming into being at the level of thought and the divine coming into being through us.

Instead of searching for the fixed beacons of first-chakra security (be they lighthouses, RFID radio pulses, or a protective father or mother god) we will discover that we are all the same one Light radiating out into the world through different-colored filters. Instead of trying out alternative personalities online or in cyberspace games, we will experience the unity behind all personalities. It is time, Anodea Judith urges us, to see ourselves as parts of an intelligent web, no longer dependent children, or dangerously independent adolescents, but "inter-dependent adults," dreaming a new dream.[45]

From this place, we will be able to download divine energy, knowledge, and intuition from the universal field. We will learn, like the spread-spectrum radios we have constructed, to receive information through multiple channels. Attachment to one channel, one belief system, one definition of "self," will no longer work in a universe of multiple vibrating beings. In seventh-level awareness, we will discover that "the angels have no actual harps; they themselves are the harps."[46] And we, emulating the angels, can also set ourselves vibrating, using sound and light practices that, like the seed programs of grid computing, open our consciousness to higher-order signals.[47] Seventh-level communications yoga will focus on downloading from the supercelestial realms the attributes—and the strength—needed for stepping up to the next level of our personal and planetary digital dharma.

The Web of the Divine[48]

Close your eyes and allow your attention to settle inside. Let your body relax, dropping your shoulders and softening your face. Focus on your breath until your mind becomes quiet, using whatever meditation techniques you are familiar with to enter a meditative state.

Allow yourself to become aware of the murmur of your own thoughts. Do not get involved in the meaning or content of those thoughts, but use sixth-level awareness to merely observe the codes of the consciousness that is thinking those thoughts. Imagine that consciousness as a bright glow of light growing stronger and brighter as you focus on it. See that light sending out ripples of energy in all directions, while staying focused on its center.

Now extend your awareness to any other person (or animal) that might be in the room with you or in the house or building in which you sit. See each of them with a center of consciousness, glowing with light just like your own, connected to you and each other by a thin line of energy.

Now extend your awareness beyond the building you are in and out to the street or countryside. Imagine the whirling points of consciousness of each sentient being in the immediate area, each as a point of light, connected to each other by thin glowing lines of energy.

See these points emanating out in all directions, with each node of consciousness as a bright light in a glowing web. Now see that web extending beyond the immediate area, to the entire town or city around you. Imagine all the points of light, representing each center of consciousness, connecting up into the web of lights that you have already imagined emanating from your own consciousness.

Now extend your awareness to increasingly larger areas around you, imagining each point of individual consciousness turning on like a light and connecting up with each other in an ever-growing web. Continue to extend this awareness until you can imagine this web of consciousness extending all around the globe, glowing with points of light for each city, country, or continent.

When you can imagine the entire web wrapping the globe, reach into your heart and allow the energy from the heart to feel your highest desire for the healing of our world. Let that feeling rise up into a prayer in the throat. Imagine uttering that prayer into the web, seeing it turn to sparkles of light that flicker through the web in all directions around you.

See that prayer being answered by the field of universal consciousness that is the Divine. Imagine that response being a new operating program from the Divine, a "seed program" that will always connect to the Source, no matter what or where the individual consciousness may be. See that program spread through the web until you can sense that it goes all around the globe. See new thoughts of healing emanating from all the nodes on the network, see them coming back to you, joining your original thought that has now completed its journey.

See the entire web glowing with the light of consciousness, growing brighter with your blessings.

A Closing Note

I f you've followed this journey through the Infosphere to the end, you've long since discovered that this book is not really a guide to the chakras or to the sociology of the media. What I have offered is a tour through the projection of human consciousness into the creation and use of our networks of communications. Standing back from our immersion in the Infosphere, I've suggested that we look at both the picture and the frame of each technology with an integral eye, seeing in each a new variation of the dance of light and shadow that is the human journey; seeing in each an opportunity to become just a little more conscious.

Simply recognizing the path of consciousness through the metaphors of telecommunications, or even practicing the kind of mindfulness suggested in this book at each level, will not, of itself, take anyone any closer to their goals of inner growth. That kind of growth requires active pursuit of an actual practice for spiritual development, often with the guidance of a teacher. Using the electronic web, even with the highest consciousness, cannot replace the energetic flow of face-to-face communications and the "social intelligence" that comes from looking into each other's eyes.

However, I do believe that by consciously looking at how we use our new communications tools, we not only open new pathways of understanding, but also build the "moral muscles" that are required to navigate the challenges of bringing forth a truly connected universe. In our daily communications with family, friends, and workmates, we can ask ourselves, "What chakra am I using right now?" and "Am I open and clear in *all* my centers?" And, when we discover that this is not the case (after all, we *are* human), we can direct our loving attention to the center that needs work. Looking outward to our role as citizens, we cannot abandon our networks to the forces of fear and the metrics of the marketplace. Instead, we must demand that each media technology be put to its best use, which requires that we recognize—before the engineers and the politicians proceed too far—the door to spiritual shadow that lies encoded in each.

The challenges of our global digital dharma are not minor. As we expand our ability to communicate from our outer selves, we face the danger of overwhelming our inner core values. The power of our tools always seems to be one step ahead of our interior moral development. In the consequences arising from our inability to control atomic weaponry and our inappropriate use of genetic engineering and nanotechnology (to give only two examples), our race is facing a crisis of extreme proportions that can only be met by strengthening our deepest core wisdom.

We cannot stop the process of interconnectivity. We are joining our individual sensory systems into greater and greater networks, into some yet-to-be-understood global intelligence. It is my hope that as we embrace the spiritual metaphors of the Infosphere as our dharma teachers, we will begin to activate the higher centers of both our individual and our collective nervous systems, thus fulfilling, together, our digital future.

NOTES

For many of the Web-based sources cited, no date could be identified. Where a date was available, it has been noted. Also, in Web sources quoted verbatim, grammatical infelicities in the original were, of course, retained.

PREFACE

1. See the bibliography for influential works by Elgin, de Quincey, Rheingold, Russell, Talbot, White, and Wilber.

INTRODUCTION

1. The term *noosphere* derives from *nous*, the Greek word for "mind." Teilhard de Chardin saw an evolutionary process of "collective cerebralisation" leading to the next stage of species evolution: the development of a "super-organism" of global intelligence. See Pierre Teilhard de Chardin, *Man's Place in Nature*, trans. René Hague (New York: Harper Colophon, 1966), chap. 4 and 5, and "The Noosphere: Verification of a Hypothesis," in *Let Me Explain*, trans. René Hague (New York: Harper & Row, 1970), 51. The "etheric body" is understood as the sustaining force field that surrounds all living beings.

2. Marshall McLuhan, *Understanding Media: The Extensions of Man* (New York: McGraw Hill, 1964), 348.

3. Ibid., 247.

4. George Carlin, *Brain Droppings* (New York: Hyperion Press, 1997), 42.

5. See for example Lewis Mumford, *Technics and Civilization* (New York: Harcourt, Brace & World, 1963), and Peter L. Berger, Brigitte Berger, and Hansfried Kellner, *The Homeless Mind: Modernization and Consciousness* (New York: Vintage, 1974).

6. Plato, *Phaedrus*, trans. R. Hackforth, in *Plato: The Collected Dialogues*, ed. Edith Hamilton and Huntington Cairns (Princeton: Princeton University Press, 1989), Sec. 275, 520. Erik Davis, *TechGnosis: Myth, Magic, and Mysticism in the Age of Information* (New York: Harmony Books, 1988).

7. Jeffrey Sconce, *Haunted Media: Electronic Presence from Telegraphy to Television* (Durham, NC: Duke University Press, 2000), 7. Vincent Mosco places our current fascination with cyberspace in a political and economic context, exploring the myths that drive each new communications technology: see Vincent Mosco, *The Digital Sublime: Myth, Power and Cyberspace* (Cambridge, MA: MIT Press, 2004). Mosco's chapter 5 summarizes the utopian promises associated with the telegraph, electricity, radio, television, and the Internet.

8. The term *meme* was coined by Richard Dawkins; it refers to a unit of cultural information transferable from one mind to another. The media as a deadly "mulligan stew" is expressed in William Irwin Thompson, *Coming Into Being: Artifacts and Texts in the Evolution of Consciousness* (New York: St. Martin's Press, 1966), 224; the warning about "colonization" is from Peter D. Hershock, *Reinventing the Wheel: A Buddhist Response to the Information Age* (Albany: SUNY Press, 1999). Another negative view is in Marie Winn, *The Plug-In Drug* (New York: Viking, 1985); two positive views are expressed in David Ronfeldt and John Arquilla, "From Cyberspace to the Noosphere: Emergence of the Global Mind," *New Perspectives Quarterly* 17, no. 1 (Winter 2000), 18, and in Let Davidson, "Cyberspace Satsang: Speculations on a Guru for the 21st Century," *Journal of the Integral Yoga of Sri Aurobindo and the Mother* 23, no. 1 (Fall 1997), http://www.collaboration.org/97/nov/text/8_cyberspace.html (previously published in *Noumenon*, Summer 1995).

9. Walter Ong first argued for the impact of media technology on individual identity and cultural formation: see Walter J. Ong, *Orality and Literacy* (New York: Methuen and Co., 1987).

10. Howard Rheingold, "Thinking About Thinking About Technology," *Noetic Science Review* 47 (Autumn-Winter 1998), 12.

11. Jennifer Cobb, *Cybergrace: The Search for God in the Digital World* (New York: Crown, 1998), 118.

12. Ibid.

13. Hermetic (the term derives from Hermes Trismegistus, purported author of a body of "ancient writings") and alchemical practices were frowned upon by the Church and thus driven "underground." The idea of an interrelationship between technology and our inner life is not new. Leonard Shlain has made the connections between modern art and physics and between the technologies of literacy and the explosion of patriarchal values: see, respectively, *Art*

and Physics: Parallel Visions of Space, Time and Light (New York: William Morrow, 1991) and *The Alphabet Versus the Goddess* (New York: Viking-Penguin, 1998). Contemporary critics Erik Davis, Jeffrey Sconce, and Michel Bauwens have drawn our attention to the inner metaphors of communications technologies: Davis, *TechGnosis*; Sconce, *Haunted Media*; Michel Bauwens, "Spirituality and Technology: Exploring the Relationship," *First Monday* 1, no. 5 (November 4, 1996), http://www.firstmonday.org/issues/issue5/bauwens/. Bauwens makes the point that our media has affected not just our external "systems of governance, economy, and social organization," but also our internal "systems of self, our individual inner values, desires, [and] motivations." I agree with this inner/outer connection. I also believe that the impacts of our telecommunications systems on our inner life are multidimensional and two-way in nature.

14. Lonny Brown, "Does the Internet Have Buddha Nature?" *CyberSangha: The Buddhist Alternative* Journal, Spring 1996, 14. The Dharma is one of the "Three Jewels" of Buddhism: the Buddha (mind's perfection of enlightenment), the Dharma (teachings and methods), and the Sangha (awakened beings who provide guidance and support): see Wikipedia contributors, "Dharma," *Wikipedia, The Free Encyclopedia*, section on "Qualities of Buddha Dharma," http://en.wikipedia.org/w/index.php?title=Dharma&oldid=1096 45331#Qualities_of_Buddha_Dharma.

15. Ken Wilber, *The Spectrum of Consciousness* (Wheaton, IL: Quest Books, 1977), 43–44; Ken Wilber, *A Theory of Everything* (Boston: Shambhala, 2000), 42–43. Wilber finds the teachings comprising the perennial wisdom path in the *Vedas* of Hinduism, in ancient Chinese medicine texts, in Tibetan Buddhism, in the "ten attributes" or *Sephiroth* of Jewish Kabbalistic teachings, and in the Christian mysticism of Teilhard de Chardin. Following Wilber's "four quadrants" approach, I have placed our telecommunications systems (as technological "extensions" of our nervous systems) in the realm of objective reality, in the upper right "exterior-individual" quadrant. Media scholars have done a good job of mapping the changes in this quadrant to their social and political impacts in the lower right "exterior-collective" holon, and to the changes in the arts and popular culture and in the lower left "interior-collective" quadrant. I have followed their lead by including how we have organized and *used* each medium in the lower right quadrant and by also discussing the dominant psychological and spiritual associations—the "inner cultural truth" or belief system, corresponding to the upper left "interior-individual" quadrant—associated with each technology. For an extended view of this four-quadrant approach, see Ken Wilber, *A Brief History of Everything*, 2nd ed. (Boston: Shambhala, 2002), chap. 4. See also his Web site, "Ken Wilber Online," especially "Excerpt G: Toward a Comprehensive Theory of Subtle Energies, Part I. Introduction: From the Great Chain of Being to Postmodernism in Three Easy Steps, http://wilber.shambhala.com/html/

books/kosmos/excerptG/part1.cfm/. Brad Reynolds presents a detailed summary of Wilber's "all quadrants, all levels" model in *Where's Wilber At? Ken Wilber's Integral Vision in the New Millennium* (St. Paul, MN: Paragon House, 2006), chap. 8 and 9.

16. The best description of all these systems is in Ken Wilber's *Integral Psychology: Consciousness, Spirit, Psychology, Therapy* (Boston: Shambhala, 2000), especially his charts starting on page 197. Elgin's model of evolution is, in his words, drawn from "the Western psychology of Mihaly Csikszentmihalyi; the spectrum psychology of Ken Wilber; the philosophy and history of human consciousness of Jean Gebser; the humanistic psychology of Abraham Maslow; the Hindu philosophy and meditative insights of Sri Aurobindo; and a range of Buddhist traditions": see Duane Elgin, *Awakening Earth: Exploring the Evolution of Human Culture and Consciousness* (New York: William Morrow, 1993), appendix 1, 319. Examples of these cited works are Abraham Maslow, *Toward a Psychology of Being* (New York: Van Nostrand Reinhold, 1989); Wilber, *Integral Psychology*; and Michael Murphy, *The Future of the Body* (Los Angeles: Jeremy Tarcher, 1992).

17. Susan G. Shumsky, *Exploring Chakras: Awaken Your Untapped Energy* (Franklin Lakes, NJ: New Page Books, 2003); Caroline Myss, *Working With Your Chakras, Archetypes, and Sacred Contracts* (Carlsbad, CA: Hay House, 2001); Anodea Judith, *Eastern Body Western Mind: Psychology and the Chakra System as a Path to Self* (Berkeley: Celestial Arts, 1996). For an online summary and links to sources about the chakras, search on "chakra" at Answers.com, http://www.answers.com. Matthew Fox has used the seven chakras as mirrors of the Christian "seven deadly sins" and their transformative opposites: see Matthew Fox, *Sins of the Spirit, Blessings of the Flesh: Lessons for Transforming Evil in Soul and Society* (New York: Harmony Books, 1999).

18. Satprem [Bernard Enginger], *Sri Aurobindo, or The Adventure of Consciousness* (New York: Institute for Evolutionary Research, 1984), 128.

19. I will reference the social memes associated with the different levels of the Spiral Dynamics model throughout this work. This system seeks to locate the core world views, or belief structures, that underlie different cultures across time and across the planet. Each of the eight core "values memes" have been given a color ranging from beige through turquoise. The externally focused Spiral Dynamics color spectrum aligns well with the inner-development focus of the ladder of consciousness. See Don Beck and Christopher Cowan, *Spiral Dynamics: Mastering Values, Leadership, and Change* (Oxford: Blackwell, 1996). On *nafs* see Shaikh Tosun Bayrak al-Jerrahi, "The Seven Levels of Being," http://www.crescentlife.com/spirituality/seven_levels.htm (2000). For Leary's circuits of consciousness, see Robert Anton Wilson, "Timothy Leary's Eight Circuits of Consciousness," Web site of Deoxy.org, http://deoxy.org/8circuit.htm, originally presented in Robert Anton Wilson, *Cosmic Trigger*,

Vol. 1, *Final Secret of the Illuminati* (Berkeley, CA: And/Or Press, 1977), and a version by "Seeker1," "A Model of the Brain in Eight Circuits According to Robert Anton Wilson and Timothy Leary," Electronic Frontiers Foundation archive, http://www.eff.org/Net_culture/Consciousness/wilson_leary _brain.model.

FIRST-LEVEL

1. Duane Elgin summarizes this stage with references to Ken Wilber's "typhonic self," Abraham Maslow's "physical needs" level, and Jean Gebsner's "magical consciousness." See Elgin, *Awakening Earth*, appendix 1, 3. Beck and Cowan (*Spiral Dynamics*) associate this with the beige "survivalistic" values.

2. Many religious traditions tell us that this desire to be *known* is what drives Spirit to manifest itself as matter, as both wave (the Hebrew *shemayim*) and as particle (*aretz*): Neil Douglas-Klotz, *The Sufi Book of Life* (New York: Penguin Compass, 2005), 36. For a discussion of quantum collapse from potentiality to physicality, see Amit Goswami, *The Self-Aware Universe: How Consciousness Creates the Material World* (Los Angeles: Jeremy P. Tarcher, 1993), and also Ervin Laszlo, *Science and the Akashic Field: An Integral Theory of Everything* (Rochester, VT: Inner Traditions, 2004), chap. 5.

3. Ervin Laszlo, *Science and the Akashic Field*, 85.

4. Sigmund Freud, *Civilization and Its Discontents* (1929; repr. London: Hogarth, 1969); Norman O. Brown, *Life Against Death: The Psychoanalytic Meaning of History* (New York: Viking, 1959); Ernst Becker, *Escape from Evil* (New York: The Free Press, 1975). The levels of "relational exchange" (used at the beginning of each subsequent chapter) are taken from Ken Wilber, *The Atman Project: A Transpersonal View of Human Development* (Wheaton, IL: Quest Books, 1980), and Wilber, *Integral Psychology*.

5. Fox, *Sins of the Spirit*, 177.

6. On *Hineini* in daily life, see Norman J. Cohen, *Hineini in Our Lives: Learning How to Respond to Others through Fourteen Biblical Texts and Personal Stories*, (Woodstock, VT: Jewish Lights, 2004).

7. Flash Rosenberg, "The Riddle of Hebrew School," Web site of Generation J, August 2001, http://www.generationj.com/archive/08_2001/riddle_hebrew _school.html. Used with permission.

8. These "touching proclamations" are cited by Randall Packer, "Eulogy for the Utopian Dream of the Net," Walker Art Center, Minneapolis, MN, 2000, http:// gallery9.walkerart.org/printtext.html?id=146&type=text&bookmark=1. For more utopian language associated with the transatlantic cable, see Tom Standage, *The Victorian Internet: The Remarkable Story of the Telegraph and the 19th Century's On-Line Pioneers* (New York: Walker and Co., 1998).

9. Nathaniel Hawthorne, *The House of the Seven Gables, A Romance* (Boston: Ticknor, Reed & Fields, 1851; London: Bohn, 1851), text from SparkNotes study guide, http://pd.sparknotes.com/lit/sevengables/section18.html.

10. Statistics from 1880 cited by Standage, *The Victorian Internet*, 102.

11. John Durham Peters, *Speaking into the Air: A History of the Idea of Communications* (Chicago: The University of Chicago Press, 1999), 139.

12. Marshall McLuhan, *Understanding Media*, 252.

13. In February 1905, a New York company created one of the first mobile broadcast stations by equipping a sedan with a wireless set to broadcast stock quotes to brokers' offices in the Wall Street area: see Douglas, *Inventing American Broadcasting*, 93. See also Mosco, *The Digital Sublime*, 120, and Sconce, *Haunted Media*, 61–64.

14. Jeffrey Sconce, *Haunted Media*, chap. 1. According to John Durham Peters, "Spiritualism was one of the chief sites at which the cultural and metaphysical implications of new forms of communication were worked out": see *Speaking into the Air*, 100. On selling radio stock to Christian Scientists, see Susan Douglas, *Inventing American Broadcasting, 1899–1922* (Baltimore: Johns Hopkins University Press, 1987), 175.

15. Susan Douglas, *Inventing American Broadcasting*, 200.

16. G. E. C. Wedlake, *SOS: The Story of Radio Communication* (New York: Crane, Russak, 1973), 57. The story of SOS is also summarized by Nautical Know How, Inc., "What is the Meaning of SOS?" 2000, http://www.boatsafe.com/nauticalknowhow/060199tip6.htm. Later, the metaphor of sending out a pulse of aliveness and waiting for a response was extended to microsecond intervals (via microwave frequencies) with the invention of radar. Its "ping, ping" pulses first guided military operations in World War II and later, after the war, civilian traffic in all forms.

17. According to energy yoga teachings, *kundalini* is a serpent wrapped around the first chakra. Intense yoga practices can release this energy up through (and thus clearing and energizing) the chakras. Poet Andrei Codrescu surmises that Tesla himself may have experienced the disturbing rush of *kundalini* in his own "light-flooded brain." See Andrei Codrescu, "Nikola Tesla's Brain," *Gambit Weekly*, February 24, 2004, http://www.bestofneworleans.com/dispatch/2004-02-24/penny.html.

18. Cited in Margaret Cheney, *Tesla: Man Out of Time* (New York: Dorset Press, 1981), 178.

19. On a more serious note, many religious organizations are sending inspirational messages and scriptural quotations to their members via SMS: "A Spiritual Connection," *The Economist,* March 12, 2005, Special Telecommunications Section, 12.

20. Maureen Dowd, "Death by Instant Message," *New York Times*, October 7, 2006, A27. Many BlackBerry users call their PDAs "CrackBerrys"—harder to quit using than stopping smoking. "Bless the Blackout," editorial, New York Times, April 21, 2007, A24.

21. Howard Rheingold, *Smart Mobs: The Next Social Revolution* (Cambridge, MA: Perseus, 2002).

22. SMS is now being used by major television networks in Europe to extend the popularity of television shows—and at the same time generate surprising revenues. For instance, a 30-second crossword quiz from CCRTV Interactiva in Spain generated 6,000 SMS answers per day, with a peak of 43,000 on a special anniversary edition—and SMS revenues ended up covering the entire cost of the television station. Similarly, a German television show, "Jede Sekunde zählt" (Every Second Counts), generated 1.2 million SMS within half an hour. See Kevin Reichard, "TV and SMS: A Perfect Match?" EarthWeb Network, http://www.instantmessagingplanet.com/wireless/article.php/1453121 (August 27, 2002).

23. Matt Richtel, "All Thumbs, Without the Stigma," *New York Times*, August 12, 2004, Circuits Section, E1.

24. "A Personal Computer To Carry In a Pocket," *New York Times*, January 8, 2007, C3.

25. Charles McGrath, "The Pleasures of the Text," *New York Times Magazine*, January 22, 2006, 15.

26. According to Australian media, one of that country's largest cellular providers discovered that "9 out of 10 teens admit they flirt by text; 53 percent had used text to ask someone out because they saw a text message as far less embarrassing than a face-to-face encounter; one in four thought it would help them 'score' because texting allows you to be more forward than when you're talking face to face": see "Text and the City," *Sidney (Australia) Morning Herald,* March 3, 2003, http://www.smh.com.au/articles/2003/03/02/10465400750 42.html?oneclick=true. For downloadable "booty calls," see the Comedy Central Web site, http://www.comedycentral.com/mobile/text_alerts/index.jhtml. On the Foley SMS scandal, see Robert McMillan, "Foley Scandal Lessons: Manage IM Use," *InfoWorld*, November 15, 2006, http://www.infoworld.com/article/06/11/15/HNfoleylessons_1.html?COLLABORATION.

27. Amy Harmon, "Internet Gives Teenage Bullies Weapons to Wound From Afar," *New York Times,* August 26, 2004, A1.

28. Bill Bryson, *A Short History of Nearly Everything* (New York: Broadway Books, 2003), 379; R. P. Bajpai, "Implications of Biophotons and Their Coherent Nature," International Institute of Biophysics Conference on Bio-photons, Moscow, Russia, September 6–10, 1999, http://www.lifescientists.de/ib_004e1.htm.

29. Michael Fitzgerald, "When Germs Talk, Maybe Humans Can Answer," *New York Times*, February 25, 2007, http://www.nytimes.com/2007/02/25/business/yourmoney/25proto.html; "Do Bacteria Sing? Sonic Intercellular Communications between Bacteria," *Molecular Microbiology* (May 1997), 879–80, cited in Howard Bloom, *The Global Brain: The Evolution of Mass Mind from the Big Bang to the 21st Century* (New York: Wiley, 2000), 17.

30. Otto Pohl, "What: Mob Scene. Who: Strangers. Point: None," *New York Times,* August 4, 2003, A4.

31. Cathy Hong, "New Political Tool: Text Messaging," *Christian Science Monitor*, June 30, 2005, http://www.csmonitor.com/2005/0630/p13s01-stct.html. Used with permission.

32. "On January 20, 2001 . . . tens of thousands of Filipinos converged on Epifanio de los Santas Avenue, known as 'Edsa' within an hour of the first volleys: 'Go 2lESDA, WEAR BLK.' Over four days, more than a million citizens showed up, mostly dressed in black. Estrada fell." Rheingold, *Smart Mobs*, 157. The Textually.org Web site has a special section on "SMS and Politics": see http://www.textually.org/textually/archives/cat_sms_and_politics.htm.

33. "Venezuela: Dial-a-protest Venezuela-style," description of segment in *Seeing Is Believing: Handicams, Human Rights, and the News, Episode 1*, documentary directed by Katerina Cizek and Peter Wintonick (Autumn 2002), http://www.seeingisbelieving.ca/cell/caracas/.

34. "Flash Mobs, Doonesbury Style," September 08, 2003, archived at http://cheesebikini.com/archives/000756.html; "Bikes Against Bush" Web site, http://bikesagainstbush.com/.

35. The tag contains a transponder with a digital memory chip that is given a unique electronic product code. The interrogator, an antenna packaged with a transceiver and decoder, emits a signal that activates the RFID tag so the interrogator can read and write data to the tag. When an RFID tag passes through the electromagnetic zone, the tag detects the reader's activation signal. The reader decodes the data encoded in the tag's integrated circuit and passes the data to the host computer for processing.

36. Mark Roberti, "Your Inventory Wants to Talk to You," *Business2.0* (May 2002), http://www.timeinc.net/b2/subscribers/articles/print/0,17925,514652,00.html; Gardiner Harris, "Tiny Antennas to Keep Tabs on US Drugs," *New*

York Times, November 15, 2004, A1.

37. Joshua Freund, "Wee-Fi," *Wired*, September 2004. For the story of the backlash against RFID badges at Brittan Elementary School, see David Kushner, "Tagging Kids Like Cattle," *Wired*, June 2005, 95.

38. Cynthia Fox, "Technogenarians," *Wired*, November 2001, http://www.wired.com/wired/archive/9.11/aging.html.

39. "RFID (Radio Frequency Identification) tags also have the ability of recording information such as details of the transactions the paper note has been involved in. It would, therefore, also prevent money-laundering, make it possible to track illegal transactions and even prevent kidnappers demanding unmarked bills," according to Prianka Chopra, an analyst with market research firm Frost and Sullivan: see Winston Chai, "Euro Notes May Be Radio Tagged," Web site of ZDNet.co.uk, May 22, 2003, http://news.zdnet.co.uk/business/0,39020645,2135074,00.htm.

40. GPS works on the principle of "trilateration." The receiver tunes to the radio signals of three (of more than two dozen) satellites of known location and distance from the earth, and then it calculates its own location on the basis of the known points in the sky. The same technique is used for cellphone location, using the angles to cell towers instead of satellites.

41. Sam Lubell, "An Electronic Tag for the Peripatetic Pet," *New York Times*, April 23, 2003, G1; Anne Eisenberg, "For the Fretting Pet Owner, A Wireless Signal," *New York Times*, July 15, 2004, Circuits Section, E8; John Markoff, "Apple Co-Founder Creates Electronic ID Tags," *New York Times*, July 21, 2003, C3. In July 2004, Mexico's attorney general "had an RFID chip implanted in his arm that can track and authenticate him, [in] a bold bid to fight government corruption": see Bruce Sterling, "Dumbing Down Smart Objects," *Wired*, October 2004, 128.

42. For example, "Teen Arrive Alive" of Bradenton, Florida, lets parents track their teens who have Nextel GPS-enabled phones. If the teen is in a car, parents can even see how fast the vehicle is traveling: see Janet Kornblum, "Prying Eyes are Everywhere," *USA Today Online*, posted April 13, 2005, http://www.usatoday.com/tech/news/2005-04-13-spyware_x.htm. Verizon Wireless offers "Chaperone," a service that, in addition to telling you the location of your child, can be programmed to provide "geo-fencing" alerts: see Matt Richtel, "Selling Surveillance to Anxious Parents," *New York Times,* May 3, 2006, E6. For a summary of phones available for Christmas 2006, see David Pogue, "Cellphones that Track the Kids," *New York Times,* December 21, 2006. Law enforcement officials are relying more and more on cellphone tracking to thwart drug deals and other crimes, but not without civil liberties challenges: see Matt Richtel, "Live Tracking of Mobile Phones Prompts Court Fights on Privacy," *New York Times*, December, 10, 2005, A1.

43. Bob Tedeschi, "You May See a Soul Mate Across a Crowded Room," *New York Times*, May 22, 2003, G3.

44. On dating, see Ryan Kim, "Hey Baby, Want a Date," *San Francisco Chronicle*, July 23, 2005, http://www.sfgate.com/cgi-bin/article.cgi?f=/c/a/2005/07/23/BUGKMDSB4P1.DTL. "Blue Tooth, a short-range signaling technology originally designed to eliminate wires between cellphones, headsets, and PDAs, has also become a flirting aid. Instead of sending electronic business cards to nearby contacts, 'Bluejackers' in Europe send racy pictures and prank messages to any phone nearby left in 'discoverable mode'": see Rachael Dodes, "When a Stranger Calls, From Afar or Nearby," *New York Times,* Circuits Section, March 24, 2005.

45. For a fear-based look at RFID, see Katherine Albrecht and Liz McIntyre, *Spychips: How Major Corporations and the Government Plan to Track Your Every Move with RFID* (Nashville, TN: Thomas Nelson, 2005). Numerous Christian Web sites debate whether RFID is the "mark of the devil"; see for example Terry Watkins, "Is the Biochip the Mark of the Beast?" Web site of 666 Watch, http://www.av1611.org/666/biochip.html.

46. On the monitoring of the oceans, see the University of Washington's NEPTUNE project, http://www.neptune.washington.edu/index.html. Responding to a call by the Viridian Institute (http://www.viridiandesign.org), a cyber-ecology organization created by science-fiction author and journalist Bruce Sterling and others, engineers have developed an electronic "pet" that changes its behavior as home energy consumption increases. The bug communicates wirelessly with the standard fuse box. The light on its tail flashes green when power use dips below 4 amperes, yellow for 4 to 12 amperes, and red for the high-use zone above 12 amperes. As consumption increases, the bug's expression changes from a smile to a frown, and it replaces its happy purr with a sad grumble. See Jessie Scanlon, "Power Players," *Wired*, September 2001, http://www.wired.com/wired/archive/9.01/meter.html. One company has developed a "personal dashboard" that updates a set of dials representing everything from one's stock portfolio value, estimated commuting time, remaining cellphone minutes, and number of unread e-mails: see http://www.ambientdevices.com/cat/index.html.51.

47. American Sufi master Samuel Lewis ("Sufi S.A.M."), who brought the Dances of Universal Peace to the world, always stressed the importance of walking with awareness, fully connecting with the feet to the earth: see Samuel Lewis, *Spiritual Dance and Walk* (San Francisco and Novato, CA: Islamia/Prophecy Publications, 1983), 53–54. For a short history of the Dances, see "About The Dances," Web site of PeaceWorks: International Network for the Dances of Universal Peace, http://dancesofuniversalpeace.org/about.htm.

48. Eckhart Tolle, *The Power of Now* (Novato, CA: New World Library, 1999).

49. Cohen, *Hineini in Our Lives.*

50. The core ACK/NACK (acknowledged/not acknowledged) dialog goes this way: The sender sends a packet of data and waits a specific interval of time for the "acknowledged" response signal from the receiver. If the response isn't received, or if the return comes back garbled, the packet is resent.

SECOND-LEVEL

1. The "reach out" advertising campaign was first used by the phone monopoly AT&T in 1979 as part of its campaign to soften its corporate image in the face of calls for deregulation. It was so popular that AT&T Wireless resurrected it in 2003. On elemental attraction, see Bloom, *The Global Brain*, 14.

2. In Spiral Dynamics (see Introduction, note 19), this corresponds to many of the qualities of the Purple meme.

3. On the Beloved, see Douglas-Klotz, *Sufi Book of Life*, 137. In *Waking the Global Heart*, Anodea Judith calls this level of spiritual development the "Age of the Static Feminine" (Santa Rosa, CA: Elite Books, 2006).

4. Wauters, *Chakras and Their Archetypes*, 51.

5. McLuhan, *Understanding Media*, 268

6. Alexander Graham Bell's notebook entry of March 10, 1876, describes the first successful experiment with the telephone, during which he spoke through the instrument to his assistant, Thomas A. Watson, in the next room. Bell writes, "I then shouted into M [the mouthpiece] the following sentence: 'Mr. Watson—come here—I want to see you.' To my delight he came and declared that he had heard and understood what I said." See Library of Congress, "Mr. Watson, Come Here," in Reason section (Gallery A) of "American Treasures of the Library of Congress," online exhibition, http://www.loc.gov/exhibits/treasures/trr002.html.

7. Davis, *TechGnosis*, 66.

8. Kempster Miller, George Patterson, Charles Thom, Robert Millikan, and Samuel McMeen, *Cyclopedia of Telephony and Telegraphy* (Chicago: American School of Correspondence, 1919), 35. Available as e-book 16517 from Project Gutenberg, http://www.gutenberg.org/files/15617/15617-h/15617-h.htm (April 2005).

9. Paul Levinson, *The Soft Edge: A Natural History and Future of the Information Revolution* (New York: Routledge, 1997), 66; Peters, *Speaking into the Air*, 198.

10. Claude Fischer, *America Calling: A Social History of the Telephone to 1940* (Berkeley and Los Angeles: University of California Press, 1992), chap. 3.

11. The campaign that AT&T launched after 1907, however, achieved something fundamentally more important and more powerful than simply portraying the company as being nice. The company appropriated the populist rhetoric of some of its most resolute foes. From trying to control its customers, Bell now moved to talking about empowerment. The ads stressed how the telephone network gave power to all its users. See Robert MacDougall, "The People's Telephone: Technological Populism and the System Idea," *The Antenna: Newsletter of the Special Interest Group in the Society for the History of Technology*, November 2002.

12. Shlain, *The Alphabet Versus the Goddess*, 18–23.

13. Of course, this voice was carefully trained to portray the telephone network as a friendly domestic helper or electric secretary. Caroline Martel's documentary film, *The Phantom of the Operator* (2004), uses a century of archival industrial training films to honor this lost feminine voice. See the Web site for the film, http://www.artifactproductions.ca/fantome/en/film/synopsis.htm.

14. Even today in rural Bangladesh, access to a cellphone has reduced domestic violence against women, according to Swanee Hunt, originator of the Women Waging Peace Policy Commission. Village "phone ladies" have not only generated their own (albeit small) incomes, but can also use their phones to call their families and friends to complain about their husbands' bad behavior and seek support: Swanee Hunt, interview by Jean Feraca, *Here on Earth*, Wisconsin Public Radio, November 20, 2006. On the Grameen Phone program in Bangladesh, see "Asia Pacific Region Microcredit Summit (APRMS) Council Meeting of Corporations, Banks, Foundations and Philanthropists," *Microcredit Summit E-news* 2, no. 1 (2004), http://www.microcreditsummit .org/enews/2004-06_cnclmtg_01.html.

15. Robert MacDougall, "Lovers, Criminals, Pranksters: Using and Misusing the Telephone, 1876–1926," paper presented at the Popular Culture Association National Conference, April 21, 2002, New Orleans, LA.

16. Virgin Mobile of Australia has a call-blocking program that for twenty cents a number prevents you from calling the boss or your girlfriend before 6 AM. See Brendan I. Koerner, "Dialing Under the Influence," *New York Times Magazine*, December 11, 2005, 66.

17. Karen Lurie, "Driving While Distracted," posted at ScienCentralNEWS, June 29, 2004, http://www.sciencentral.com/articles/view.php3?type=article&article_id=218392289. "Hands-free" car phones, often touted as safer, appeared to be slightly more dangerous than hand-held terminals. The first research into the effects of car phones, conducted at the University of Toronto in 1997 and

published in the *New England Journal of Medicine*, compared accident reports to phone billing records: see Andy Dornan, "There Is No Information Super-highway," *Callcenter Magazine*, March 5, 2003, http://www.commweb.com/article/NMG20030305S0016. See also Jeremy Peters, "Hands-Free Cellphone Devices Don't Aid Road Safety, Study Concludes," *New York Times,* July 12, 2005, http://www.nytimes.com/2005/07/12/technology/12auto.html.

18. Account taken from a collection of cellphone accident stories on the Web site of the syndicated radio show *Car Talk.* See "Drive Now, Talk Later: Actual Driving and Talking Accidents," http://www.cartalk.com/content/features/Drive-Now/accidents-2.html. Ellipsis in original.

19. Heather Horst, "From Kinship to Link-Up: Cell Phones and Social Networking in Jamaica," *Current Anthropology* 46, no. 5 (2005), 755; Benedict Carey, "New Therapy on Depression Finds Phone is Effective," *New York Times*, August 25, 2004, A20.

20. Matt Richtel and Ken Belson, "Online Calling Heralds an Era of Lower Costs," *New York Times,* Circuits Section, July 3, 2006, A1; Ben McGrath, "Baghdad to Swarthmore," *New Yorker*, December 26, 2005, 46; Ethan Todras-Whitehall, "Internet Phone Service Creating Chatty Network," *New York Times,* Circuits Section, March 24, 2005.

21. In Europe, people spend over $100 million a year for pornography via cell-phone, and the U.S. market is estimated to grow to be twice that by 2009: see Matt Richtel and Michel Marriot, "Ring Tones, Cameras, Now This: Sex is Latest Cellphone Feature," *New York Times*, September 17, 2005, A1.

22. Daniel J. Czitrom, *Media and the American Mind: From Morse to McLuhan* (Chapel Hill: University of North Carolina Press, 1982), 67. Quotation from *Century Magazine* (March 1902), 782, cited in Douglas, *Inventing American Broadcasting*, 24.

23. *New York Times*, January 23, 1910, Sect. 5, 6, as cited in Douglas, *Inventing American Broadcasting*, 173.

24. See Yuki Noguchi, "Connecting With Kids, Wirelessly," *Washington Post,* July 7, 2005, A01, http://www.washingtonpost.com/wp-dyn/content/article/2005/07/06/AR2005070602100.html. On the new phones for the younger set, see David Pogue, "Can't Find Little Johnny? Ring His Cell," *New York Times*, Circuits Section, December 22, 2005, C1. The Walt Disney Company hopes to exploit the trend in child security phones by selling cellphone services to young children. The package of services will include both entertainment for kids and "tracking services" for parents.

25. Paul Levinson, *Cellphone: The Story of the World's Most Mobile Medium and How It Transformed Everything!* (New York: Palgrave, 2004); Elissa Gootman, "Cellphone Ban is Enforced, and Parents Howl, Too," *New York Times,* April

27, 2006, C16; Cheryl A. Barnard, "The Impact of Cellphone Use on Building Community," *Student Affairs On-line* 4, no. 4 (Fall 2003), http://www.student affairs.com/ejournal/Fall_2003/Cellphones.html. A mother's "telephone stalking" of her college-age daughter was satirized in a Roz Chast cartoon, "Someone is Out There Watching," in the *New Yorker*, January 10, 2005, available at at http://www.cartoonbank.com (search on "Chast someone watching").

26. Andrea Elliott, "Talking to Me? No, the Cabby's On His Cell," *New York Times*, July 17, 2003, 1.

27. Kevin Bishop, "Europe, Of cabbages and satellite phones," BBC News Web site, May 2, 1999, http://news.bbc.co.uk/1/hi/world/europe/334080.stm. Dennis Grey, "Internet, High-tech Tools Speed Reunions of Kosovo Families," Associated Press, June 5, 1999.

28. On cellphone growth in Africa, see Rhett Butler, "Cell Phones May Help 'Save' Africa," *New York Times*, August 25, 2005, A1, and Web site of Centre sur les politiques internationales des TIC pour l'Afrique Centrale et de l'Ouest, http://www.cipaco.org/spip.php?article1167. On cellphone impact in Senegal, see story by Nathan McClintock, "Abderahmane Sow, Agroentrepreneur, Belel, Matam Region," at Web site of The New Farm, http://www.newfarm.org/international/senegal/0106/index.shtml. On Bangladesh's "phone ladies" see chap. 2, note 14. In case you want to order a cellphone coffin for yourself, see eShop Africa at http://www.eshopafrica.com/acatalog/Ga_Coffins.html.

29. In a recent Associated Press investigation, collect calls made from California jails are charged an average of seven times as much as the same call would be charged if made from a public pay phone. These charges total about $120 million a year on the phone bills of families and friends of county jail inmates. See Charles Montaldo, "Phone Companies Rip Off Inmate Families," Crime/Punishment section of About.com Web site, http://crime.about.com/od/prison_families/a/inmate_calls.htm.

30. "The Bankrupt-Your-Family Calling Plan," editorial, *New York Times*, December 22, 2006, A30.

31. Herbert Stein, "The Sidewalk Nursery," *Slate*, posted September 18, 1998, http://slate.msn.com/id/2578/.

32. Amy Harmon, "Reach Out and Touch No One," *New York Times*, April 14, 2005, E1.

33. Keith Bradsher, "Sad, Lonely? For a Good Time, Call Vivienne," *New York Times*, February 24, 2005, C1. Vivienne has since disappeared from the Web; as of February 2007 her newer cousins can be seen at http://www.v girl.com/.

34. On mobile virtual network operators, see Wilson Rothman, "Sending the Brand into the Wireless World," *New York Times,* May 3, 2006, E6.

35. The Gartner Group estimates that over $1.2 billion was spent on ringtones and "wallpaper" for cellphones in the United States in 2004. For stories on popularity of ringtones, see Jyotti Thottam, "How Kids Set the (Ring) Tone, *Time,* April 4, 2005, and Jeff Leeds, "The Guy from Green Day Says He Has Your Mother on the Phone," *New York Times,* August 18, 2004, Business Section, 1. While most tones are tapped from commercial music sources, in many parts of the world devout high-tech Muslims can download prayer chants as well as alerts as to prayer times: see Mala Punjabi, "A High-Tech Way to Spread the Word," *Asiaweek,* December 7, 2001, 15.

36. Ethan Todards-Whitehall, "Making Connections, Here and Now," *New York Times,* January 25, 2006, E3. See also the tours at the Talking Street Web site, http://www.talkingstreet.com. Several historical sites, including Minute Man National Park, are using cellphone tours; tour descriptions are given on the park's Web site at http://www.nps.gov/mima/CELLPHONEAUDIO-TOURS.html. Portland's "Call of the Wild" tours are described at http://latteier.com/call/. The BBC project is described at "Barcodes On The Beach With BBC's New Mobile Content Service," Web site of Textually.org, July 18, 2005, http://www.textually.org/textually/archives/2005/07/009131.htm.

37. For more on entrainment, see Joshua Leeds, *Sonic Alchemy: Conversations with Leading Sound Practitioners* (Sausalito, CA: InnerSong, 1997).

THIRD-LEVEL

1. Neil Douglas-Klotz (*Sufi Book of Life,* 13) tells us that Jesus (in Matthew 6:10) spoke *teete malkutakh,* or, "let the 'I Can' of the cosmos really come!"

2. Elgin, *Awakening Earth,* appendix 1, 322. Projected outwards into society, third-chakra values are associated by Beck and Cowan with the consolidation of feudal patriarchal authority (the red values-meme) and (later) the dynamic materialism of competitive capitalism and the emergence of the national state. As third-stage societies mature (into blue meme values), once-arbitrary rules become codified in legal and moral codes, expertise is genuinely respected, and top-down order and stability reign.

3. Fox, *Sins of the Spirit,* 34.

4. Early radio pioneers spent decades trying to overcome the public nature of the radio medium. It wasn't until the 1920s that this "failing" was turned into opportunity—the new medium of broadcasting. See Sconce, *Haunted Media,* 93; Douglas, *Inventing American Broadcasting,* 33.

5. Some scientists believe the role of music in human evolutionary history was not to create social cohesion but to signal it to rival groups. By performing complicated music and dance, "a group could show it had the coordination to prevail in a scrap, and could thus avoid a fight altogether." See Nicholas Wade, "We Got Rhythm; the Mystery Is How and Why," *New York Times*, September 16, 2003, D1. See also Hadley Cantril and Gordon W. Allport, *Psychology of Radio* (New York & London: Harper & Brothers, 1935), cited in Peters, *Speaking into the Air*, 216–17. Douglas (*Inventing American Broadcasting*, 172) tells us that Lee DeForest, the inventor of the radio amplifying vacuum tube, first thought of broadcasting as way of delivering the opera.

6. Czitrom, *Media and the American Mind*, 81. For a discussion of these cases and the decline of educational radio, see Eric Barnouw, *A History of Broadcasting in the United States*, vols. 1 and 2 (New York: Oxford University Press, 1966, 1968), and Robert W. McChesney, *Telecommunications, Mass Media and Democracy: The Battle for the Control of US Broadcasting, 1928–1935* (New York: Oxford University Press, 1993).

7. I attended a 2006 Wisconsin Book Festival presentation at which Wisconsin Public Radio (WPR) historian Randall Davidson told us about one rural school whose classroom radio stopped working one morning. The frantic teacher took her class out to the highway and waved down the first car they saw with a radio antenna. The driver opened all the doors and the children gathered around so that they could sing along with WHA (Madison's) "Journeys in Musicland." See Randall Davidson, *9XM Talking: WHA Radio and the Wisconsin Idea* (Madison, University of Wisconsin Press, 2006). For audio clips from some of these programs, see Randall Davidson, "Wisconsin School of the Air Expanded Students' Horizons through Radio," at the PortalWisconsin.org Web site, http://www.portalwisconsin.org/wsahistoryfeature.cfm.

8. Long advocated "a populist program for redistributing wealth through sharply graduated income and inheritance taxes. As his national recognition (and ambitions) grew, he spoke with increasing frequency to national radio audiences. No politician in this era—except Roosevelt himself and Long's sometime ally, Father Charles Coughlin—used radio as frequently and effectively." See "'Share the Wealth': Huey Long Talks to the Nation," History Matters: The U.S. Survey Course on the Web, http://historymatters.gmu.edu/d/5109/. Father Coughlin's radio sermons in the 1930s attracted more than 40 million listeners. While he defended the "little man," Coughlin's talks increasingly took on a nasty edge as he combined harsh attacks on Roosevelt as the tool of international Jewish bankers with praise for the fascist leaders Benito Mussolini and Adolph Hitler. See "'Somebody Must be Blamed': Father Coughlin Speaks to the Nation," History Matters: The U.S. Survey Course on the Web, http://historymatters.gmu.edu/d/5111/. On Long and

Coughlin's effective use of radio, see Alan Brinkley, *Voices of Protest* (New York: Alfred Knopf, 1982).

9. Levinson, *The Soft Edge*, 89.

10. Marc Lacey, "Mexican Protesters Try to Protect Their Rallying Cry," *New York Times*, October 30, 2006; Alexander Stille, "Cameras Shoot Where Uzis Can't," *New York Times,* Arts and Ideas Section, September 20, 2003, A15.

11. "Secret Radios Eyed for North Korea," *Japan Times*, March 25, 2003, http://search.japantimes.co.jp/cgi-bin/nn20030325b7.html (registration required); article summarized at http://www.intellnet.org/news/2003/03/24/18515-1.htm.

12. Shlain, *The Alphabet Versus the Goddess*, 404.

13. "Even more than telephone or telegraph, radio is the extension of the central nervous system that is matched only by human speech itself. . . . It provides the tight tribal bond of the world of the common market, of song, of resonance": McLuhan, *Understanding Media*, 302.

14. "Radio is the medium for frenzy, and it has been the major means of hotting up the tribal blood of Africa, India and China, alike": Ibid., 310.

15. And it is television that is helping with the healing in Yugoslavia. See next chapter.

16. The war crimes tribunal said the radio station lured victims to killing grounds and broadcast the names of people to be singled out for execution: see Sharon LaFraniere, "Court Finds Rwanda Media Executives Guilty of Genocide," *New York Times*, December 3, 2003, online edition, http://www.nytimes.com/2003/12/03/international/africa/03CND-RWAN.html?hp. The government-controlled media in Zimbabwe were "accomplices to murder" according to the Harare-based Media Monitoring Project Zimbabwe, the country's independent media watchdog: see "State Media Spews 'Hate Speech,'" News24.com, December 20, 2003, http://www.news24.com/News24/Archive/0,,2-1659_1461741,00.html.

17. While the Al Jazeera television network has aired clerics calling for jihad, it does so under the guise of "news." For an example of a fundamentalist radio station, see Chris Johnston, "Call to Close Down London-based Arabic Radio Station," *Guardian* (UK), online edition, August 18, 2005, http://politics.guardian.co.uk/media/story/0,12123,1551556,00.html

18. Sam Phillips introducing Elvis Presley, as recalled by band member Charlie Feathers; see "Charlie Feathers Speaks," dated 1979, Web site of Rockabilly Hall of Fame, http://www.rockabillyhall.com/CharlieSpeaks.html.

19. Radio historian Dave Marsh writes that in many Black communities in the early years of the civil rights movement, local AM radio was used as a secret

call to protest, providing young listeners "coded messages about where to gather for illegal demonstrations." Local Spanish-language disc jockeys, he says, played the same role four decades later "in delivering hundreds of thousands of immigration-rights supporters into the streets of Los Angeles and other cities." See David Marsh, "Radio Days," *New York Times Book Review*, January 28, 2007, 11.

20. As is the case with most protest music, market forces soon seized upon this widely popular new musical form. On commercial radio, strutting verses about tribal gang violence, money, and sex sadly soon replaced much of its original political content. On stealing electrical power, see Anonymous, "I must correct Parris . . . ", posted to History of Hip Hop thread, Black Roots Village forum, at The Black Forum - The Blacknet Village, February 24th, 2005, at 13:00, http://www.blackchat.co.uk/theblackforum/forum37/9023.html. For Los Angeles rapper "Amad Jamal," see interview with Phatmag at http://www.phatmag.com/Mag%20Pages/Articles/07_04_01/AJ/AJ_inter.html. Taking back the streets, as opposed to atomized private listening, is still one of the rallying cries of "political hip hop": see Adam Mansbach, "Technology and Race at the Millennium: An Interview with Professor Tricia Rose," http://www.adammansbach.com/other/interview-tricia.html.

21. On third-chakra communications issues, see Brad Blanton, *Radical Honesty* (New York: Dell Trade Paperback, 1996), 120–125. On the Right we see (Spiral Dynamics Blue meme) "conservative" cultures confronting (Spiral Dynamics Orange meme) individualism, a confrontation that may explain why right-wing radio was so much more successful than attempts by liberals to create their own version of "angry talk" on Air America Radio. Liberals, who believe in the liberating power of discourse, gravitate to radio for intelligent conversation by respected leaders and for community education, not for humiliation of the enemy. When Air America emulated the cynical and personal "gotcha" style of the right, it only embarrassed its audience. On the limits of left-wing approaches to radio, a good example is WBAI-FM in New York, where the station's "progressive" programming has become, according to a recent *New Yorker* article, "a Balkanized schedule of shows such as 'First Voices Indigenous Radio,' 'Out-FM,' 'Joy of Resistance' ('multicultural feminist radio'), 'Beyond the Pale' ('progressive Jewish politics'), 'The largest minority' ('issues affecting people with disabilities'), 'Afrikaleidoscope,' and 'Asia Pacific Forum.'" See Marc Fisher, "Voice of the Cabal," *New Yorker,* December 4, 2006, 60.

22. Charles C. Mann, "The Resurrection of Indie Radio," *Wired*, March 2005, 103.

23. Lee Jenkins, "Radio Days: New Technology, Old Habit," *New York Times,* July 12, 2005, C18. Jaime Wolf's "The Star Maker of the Semipopular" in the *New York Times Magazine* (June 26, 2005), profiles KCRW's Nic Harcourt, "a

Los Angeles public-radio DJ [who] became America's arbiter of cool music."
See also Lorne Manly, "As Satellite Radio Takes Off, It Is Altering the
Airwaves," *New York Times,* April 5, 2005, A1.

24. Rádio Favela is the subject of Helvécio Ratton's Brazilian film *Something in the
Air.* See interview with Misael Avelino dos Santos, "Q&A: Brazil's Pirate
Radio Pioneer: 'We Raise Consciousness,'" Resource Center of the Americas,
February 2003, http://www.americas.org/item_186.

25. "Oxygen for Youth," *Oxfam Exchange*, Spring 2003, 10. Thomas Friedman
observed that low-powered FM radio brought "low-tech democracy" to
Ghana: for "Ghana's poor, illiterate masses, being able to call the radio . . . has
given them a chance to participate in politics as never before"; see "Low-Tech
Democracy," op-ed column, *New York Times*, May 1, 2001, A23, A27. On
Israel-Palestine dialog, see the Web site of Radio All for Peace, http://www.all
forpeace.org/index.aspx?lang=en.

26. *Saq'Be*, an organization for Mayan and indigenous spiritual studies based in
Santa Fe, New Mexico, reports that in Chichicastenango, "the vast majority of
radio stations are committed to Protestant and Evangelical proselytizing, with
NO forum for the voice of the ancient traditional ways." See Admin, "Radio
Project: Securing a Means for the Traditional Mayan Voice to be Heard in
Chichicastenango, Guatemala," posted at the Web site of *Saq'Be*, September
12, 2003, http://www.sacredroad.org/article.php?story=200309121447305
94&mode=print. On community radio, see Mark Camp and Agenes
Portalewska, "A Question of Frequency: Community Radio in Guatemala,"
Cultural Survival Quarterly, Summer 2005. In the same issue, see Guy
Buchholtzer, "Missing: Where Are First Nations in National Media?"

27. Alita Edgar, "The Truth About 'Public' Radio," Mediabistro.com Web site,
April 6, 2001, http://www.mediabistro.com/feature/archives/01/04/02/; John
Anderson, "Microradio Turns 21," *The Undercurrent* (Fresno, CA), August
2006, at http://www.fresnoundercurrent.net/2006/aug/microjohn.html.

28. Sam Keen, *Fire in the Belly: On Being a Man* (New York: Bantam Doubleday,
1991). "New Warrior" training is part of the ManKind Project, http://www
.mkp.org/nw.htm.

29. While today "clear channel" is associated with a large radio ownership group,
in the early days of broadcasting it signified a station (in the AM band) that
did not have to drop its power at sunset and was thus able to reach wide
swaths of the country.

FOURTH-LEVEL

1. *Spiral Dynamics*, Beck and Cowan associate this level of idealized relationship with the egalitarian Green meme. On the dynamic feminine, see Judith, *Waking the Global Heart*, 199–211.

2. Elgin, *Awakening Earth*, appendix 1.

3. Judith, *Eastern Body Western Mind*, 278–79. On the chakra archetypes, see Wauters, *Chakras and Their Archetypes*, 91.

4. Donna Seaman, review of *Boomeritis* by Ken Wilber, *Booklist*, June 1 and 15, 2002, http://archive.ala.org/booklist/v98/je1/31wilber.html; Beck and Cowan, *Spiral Dynamics*, 266. The hunger for status goods is an Orange meme value carried into Green meme television advertising and programs built around the "lives of the rich and famous."

5. "The Playboy Interview: Marshall McLuhan," *Playboy*, March 1969.

6. As Steven Johnson reminded us about the Kennedy-Nixon debate of 1960, "Nixon lost on TV because he didn't *look* like someone we would want as president, and where emotional IQ is concerned, looks don't always deceive": see Steven Johnson, *Everything Bad is Good for You: How Today's Popular Culture is Actually Making Us Smarter* (New York: Riverhead Books, 2005), 103.

7. Spiral Dynamics' Orange and Green memes.

8. Shlain, *The Alphabet Versus the Goddess*, 408–9.

9. Elgin, *Awakening Earth*, 140.

10. They cite TV's contribution to the success of the Civil Rights movement. Paul Ray and Sherry Ruth Anderson, *The Cultural Creatives* (New York: Harmony Books, 2000).

11. Steven D. Stark, *Glued to the Set: The 60 Television Shows and Events That Made Us Who We Are Today* (New York: Free Press, 1997), 31.

12. For a loving remembrance of *Star Trek* by one of the follow-up series's writers, see Ronald Moore, "Mr. Universe," *New York Times,* September 18, 2006, A29.

13. Even though the series *Postcards from Buster* had a mandate from the Department of Education to "highlight diversity," showing a lesbian family was too much for the Department's newly appointed secretary, Margaret Spellings, who wrote a letter of condemnation to WGBH-TV/Boston, the program's producer. Covering twenty-four states, Buster has visited Hmong children, Mormons, Muslims, and evangelical Christians. See Julie Salamon, "A Child Learns a Harsh Lesson in Politics," *New York Times*, February 5, 2005, B7.

14. The effect was particularly noticeable in coverage of the Israeli occupation of Palestine, Israel's 2006 campaign against Hezbollah in southern Lebanon, and American bombing in Iraq and its deadly effects on women and children.

15. Arie Farnam, "TV Show Helps Macedonia Mend," *Christian Science Monitor*, October 9, 2003, http://www.csmonitor.com/2003/1009/p06s01-woeu.html. On *Sesame Street*, see "Rruga Sesam & Ulica Sezam—Sesame Street Kosovo," a discussion of the film *The World According to Sesame Street* on the Web site of Participate.net, http://www.participate.net/sesamestreet/kosovo. This program was featured on *Independent Lens* on many public television stations in October 2006: see "Terrence Howard to Host Fifth Season of PBS's Emmy Award-Winning Series *Independent Lens*," press release, posted at Independent Television Service, August 21, 2006, http://www.itvs.org/press room/pressRelease.htm?pressId=329. Another version of *Sesame Street* created in South Africa features a puppet character with HIV/AIDS.

16. The filmmakers have been approached by the Dutch government with the idea of expanding their project to Israel and Palestine: see Alan Riding, "In Balkans, Video Letters Reconcile Lost Friends," *New York Times*, June 9, 2005, B1.

17. David Dark, *Everyday Apocalypse* (Grand Rapids, MI: Brazos Press, 2002), 43. In Spiral Dynamics terms, this dynamic can also be understood as the self-centered Orange meme still lurking in the Green, which we see reflected in the "consume to be noticed" message of most television commercials.

18. On the "pain body" see Eckhart Tolle's *Living the Liberated Life and Dealing with the Pain Body*, audio recording (Louisville, CO: Sounds True Audio, 2001), and his book *A New Earth: Awakening to Your Life's Purpose* (New York: Dutton/Penguin, 2005).

19. Again, at its worst, television forces us to acknowledge how closely the cynicism of the Orange meme (for the failures of society) lurks under our contemporary "Green" mask of liberal compassion. On true compassion, see Fox, *Sins of the Spirit*, 251.

20. Bill McKibben, *The Age of Missing Information* (New York: Random House, 1992), 183; Erin Texeira, "Racial Unrealties," *Capital Times* (Madison WI), February 17, 2005, E1, also available as "Multiracial Scenes Now Common in TV Ads," MSNBC Web site, http://www.msnbc.msn.com/id/6975669/.

21. He was undone by the essential emptiness of television-land values. The explosion of the Internet (which indeed had been promoted by Vice President Gore, who was one of the first politicians to see the value of the Internet and supported much of the federal funding that moved the network from the control of the military into the public sphere) brought new expectations for truth-telling and new ways of catching mistruths, while the country's sense of ungroundedness in the post-Vietnam years opened the doors to a counter-retreat to the certainties of third-level moral absoluteness, remilitarization of

American foreign policy, and the regressive politics of "compassionate conservatism." Another social-political reflection of the third- and fourth-chakra split was the creation of the "all volunteer" military. Andrew Bacevich, *The New American Militarism: How Americans Are Seduced by War* (London: Oxford University Press, 2005).

22. In Spiral Dynamics terms, this is a conflict between TV's inherent Green values and its inherited commercial and government-driven Orange memes.

23. David Brooks, "Hummers to Harleys," *New York Times,* October 4, 2003, A13.

24. Media critic Christopher Orr writes that those promiscuously tortured on Fox's hit series *24* are in fact, the least likely to be abused in real life. They receive such implausible treatment in order for the show to advertise its "hard-core" nature. See Christopher Orr, "Kiefer Madness," *The New Republic*, May 15, 2006, https://ssl.tnr.com/p/docsub.mhtml?i=20060522&s=orr052206.

25. TV's extreme pairings are taken to the extreme in such shows as *Wife Swap*, which featured a lesbian mother sent to the home of a fundamentalist. The Web site for "Thirty Days" is at http://www.fxnetworks.com/shows/originals/30days/main.html.

26. Bill Buford, "TV Dinners: The Rise of Food Television," *New Yorker,* October 2, 2006, 42. In mid-2006, *New York Times* columnist Maureen Dowd observed, "As the administration has gotten more hypermasculine and martial (when will Dick Cheney order us to change all our clocks to military time?), prime time is getting more feminine and seductive": see Maureen Dowd, "From McBeal to McDreamy," *New York Times*, May 17, 2006. For a defense of this new crop of "reality" competitions see, Michael Hirschorn, "The Case for Reality TV," *Atlantic Monthly*, May 2007, 138.

27. Steven Johnson, *Interface Culture: How New Technology Transforms the Way We Create and Communicate* (New York: HarperCollins, 1997), 31.

28. On the phrase "whatever" as an existential response to a glut of mediated "options," see Thomas de Zengotita, *Mediated: How the Media Shapes Your World and the Way You Live in It* (New York: Bloomsbury Publishing, 2005). An excerpt discussing "whatever" is published at Zengotita's Web site, http://www.mediatedtdez.com/excerpts/mediatedexcerpt_sl_whatever.pdf.

29. Richard Grossinger, *On the Integration of Nature: Post 9/11 Biopolitical Notes* (Berkeley: North Atlantic Books, 2005), 209.

30. Douglas-Klotz, *Sufi Book of Life*, 221. On *metta*, see Sharon Salzberg, "Facets of Metta," Web site of Vipassana Fellowship, http://www.vipassana.com/meditation/facets_of_metta.php

FIFTH-LEVEL

1. Beck and Cowan, *Spiral Dynamics*, 274. Wilber's explanation of Spiral Dynamics' second tier can be found at "On Critics, Integral Institute, My Recent Writing, and Other Matters of Little Consequence: A Shambhala Interview with Ken Wilber," http://wilber.shambhala.com/html/interviews/interview1220.cfm/.

2. In the Spiral Dynamics framework, at this level cultures begin the move from Green to Yellow meme values, with people living easily in multiple connected networks, able to find their way in "a kaleidoscope of natural hierarchies, systems and forms": Beck and Cowan, *Spiral Dynamics*, 47, 114. See also Elgin, *Awakening Earth*, appendix 1.

3. Wilber (chap. 5, note 1) argues that "less than 2 percent of the population [is] at second-tier thinking." Christopher Cowan, splitting with his former partner Don Beck, has rejected Wilber's use of the Spiral Dynamics model and has warned against "the 'tier-anical' view [that] assigns superiority and spiritual cleverness to the 'second tier' and relegates the first tier to second-rate status, creating categories for greater and lesser mortals with the second tier nearer to transcendent being." See "What Do the Terms 'First Tier' and 'Second Tier' Signify?" in the Frequently Asked Questions section of the Spiral Dynamics Web site, http://www.spiraldynamics.org/faq_levels.htm#06.

4. Mike Stokes, "Fifth Chakra: Purpose, Truth and Choice," Web site of Freedom Yoga with Mike Stokes, http://www.freedomyoga.com/fifthchakra.htm.

5. Margaret Wertheim, *The Pearly Gates of Cyberspace* (New York: W. W. Norton, 1999), 228.

6. Francis H. Cook, *Hua-Yen Buddhism: The Jewel Net of Indra* (University Park, PA: Penn State University Press, 1977), quoted at "Indra's Net: What Is It?" on Heart Space: The Web Site of Phil Servedio, http://www.heartspace.org/misc/IndraNet.html.

7. John Lahr, "Cultural Gas," *New Yorker,* October 6, 2003, 136.

8. Brown, intro., note 14. Michael Grosso, *The Millenium Myth: Love and Death at the End of Time* (Wheaton, IL: Quest Books, 1997). For a comparison of these views, see Michel Bauwens, "Deus ex Machina vs. Electric Gaia," *Computer-Mediated Communication Magazine*, April 1997, http://www.december.com/cmc/mag/1997/apr/last.html.

9. Wertheim, *Pearly Gates of Cyberspace*, 278.

10. The Internet's transmission design appears to be a metaphor for the soul's journey. We learn by lifetimes of experience, understanding the true meaning of our karmic path only at the end of what may have appeared to be inconse-

quential choices, when so many separate life experiences are reassembled for us to understand. We can choose to act as if this life, in Sri Aurobindo's words, is "the conscious meeting place of the finite and the infinite": see Sri Aurobindo, *The Problem of Rebirth* (Pondicherry: Sri Aurobindo Ashram, 1952), 83, cited in John White, *The Meeting of Science and Spirit* (New York: Paragon House, 1990), 96.

11. Of course, the Net's structure is like an underground organization, composed of many cells connected through multiple points of contact but lacking a traditional command center: see Katie Hafner, "Internet Users Thinking Twice Before a Search," *New York Times*, January 25, 2006, A1.

12. Nicholas Kristof, "Death by a Thousand Blogs," *New York Times,* May 24, 2005, A21.

13. Blog numbers from Eric Pfanner, "55 Million Blogs, and Now a Service to Track Them," *New York Times,* October 16, 2006, http://www.nytimes.com/2006/10/16/technology/16blog.html. Another source claims 57 million or 60 million, with 17 million in China alone: see Graham Charlton, "Chinese Bloggers Reach 17 Million Mark," Web site of E-consultancy, October 9, 2006, http://www.e-consultancy.com/news-blog/361837/chinese-bloggers-reach-17-million-mark.html. For number of podcasts handled by Feed Burner, see "Podcasts Surpass Radio Stations Worldwide; Podcast Demand Growing Faster Than Supply," Podcasting News Web site, April 18, 2006, http://www.podcastingnews.com/archives/2006/04/podcasts_surpas.html.

14. Tom Zeller Jr., "The Lives of Teenagers Now: Open Blogs, Not Closed Diaries," *The New York Times*, November 3, 2005, C1. Blog count (as of May 2006) from The Blog Herald, http://www.blogherald.com/2005/05/25/worldwide-blog-count-for-may-now-over-60-million-blogs/. On blogs and elections, see Adam Cohen, "Could a 15-Year-Old With a Laptop Be the Next Campaign Media Guru?" op-ed column, *New York Times,* June 14, 2006. One middle-aged male columnist wrote that after experiencing the power of video-conferencing and YouTube, "Madonna might be scheduled to mud-wrestle Britney Spears on premium cable and I'd still probably pick video-chatting with my children": see David Carr, "Idiosyncratic and Personal, PC Edges TV," *New York Times,* October 16, 2006, C1.

15. "This new project of transmodernity implies political, economic, ecological, erotic, pedagogic, and religious liberation": see Enrique Dussel, *The Invention of the Americas: Eclipse of the Other and the Myth of Modernity* (New York: Continuum, 1995), 138, cited by Brett Greider, "Academic Buddhology and the Cyber-Sangha: Researching and Teaching Buddhism through Multimedia and Internet Sources," presentation at American Academy of Religion conference, Saint Paul, MN, April 28, 2000. Abstract at http://teaching_buddhism.tripod.com/papers.html.

16. John Markoff, a reporter for the *New York Times*, makes the case that the personal computer emerged from the same 1960s counterculture that was experimenting with psychedelic drugs and eastern religions: see John Markoff, *What the Dormouse Said: How the Sixties Counterculture Shaped the Personal Computer Industry* (New York: Viking, 2005). See also Elgin, *Awakening Earth*, 163.

17. Kevin Kelly, "Scan This Book!" *New York Times Magazine,* May 14, 2006, 44.

18. Heather Green, "Let a Million Videos Bloom Online," *Business Week*, online edition, December 29, 2004, http://www.businessweek.com/bwdaily/dnflash/dec2004/nf20041229_0845_db016.htm?campaign_id=rss_daily; Anick Jesanum, "Growing Craze: Sharing Personal Videos," *San Francisco Chronicle*, January 23, 2006, C2.

19. Police are reporting cases in which mugging victims are capturing images of their fleeing assailants on their cellphones: see Leslie Walker, "Personal Images Brought to Life," *Washington Post* story distributed by Associated Press, published in *Capital Times* (Madison, WI), December 23, 2004, 6E.

20. See chap. 5, note 4 (Stokes). One form of international fifth-chakra arrogance is the U.S. corporate dominance of the assignment of network "domain names." Many countries are demanding that they have the right to add new non-Roman letter suffixes (such as Chinese or Arabic) to the Net's "root" servers, others, such as Palestine, just want their country code (".ps") recognized; see Mosco, *The Digital Sublime*, 164. Other governments worry that the U.S. dominance of the Net will allow it to "turn off" service in countries it disagrees with—or plans to attack; see Christopher Rhoads, "In Threat to Internet's Clout, Some Are Starting Alternatives," *The Wall Street Journal,* January 19, 2006, A1.

21. Even China, with its dedicated political censors, has not been able to keep up with the sex and drug scams and the exploding youth entertainment side of the Internet; see David Barboza, "The Wild Web of China; 110 Million Surfers Can Buy Sex and Drugs, but Reform Is Still Illicit," *New York Times,* March 8, 2006, C1.

22. On "shadow side" Internet revenues, including comments by Sterling, see John Schwartz, "From Unseemly to Lowbrow, the Web's Real Money Is in the Gutter," *New York Times,* August 26, 2002.

23. "Hermes Myths 1," section "Hermes' Theft of Apollon's Cattle" (from Homeric Hymn to Hermes) at the Web site of The Theoi Project: A Guide to Greek Mythology, http://www.theoi.com/Olympios/HermesMyths.html#Theft1. For text of the Homeric Hymn to Hermes, see http://homer.thefreelibrary.com/Collection-Of-Hesiod-Homer-and-Homerica/30-1.

24. "The age of privacy is over and with it the ability to sustain denial," said Dr. Sheenah Hankin, a psychotherapist in New York City. "Anyone can search the Internet and discover a lot about their spouse." See Jane Gross, "When the Computer Opens the Closet," *New York Times,* August 22, 2004, Styles Section, 1. On college sports teams' bad behavior being "outed," see Richard Sandomir, "College Athletes Acting Badly: It's All There on the Web," *New York Times,* May 18, 2006, C18.

25. Hollywood lawyers discovered that their "cease and desist" letters to those who broke the HD encryption code generated a web rebellion, with the secret posted on dozens of websites and incorporated into songs and photos: see, Brad Stone, "In Web Uproar, Antipiracy Code Spreads Wildly," *New York Times*, May 3, 2007. A1. The Church of Scientology has been trying for years to block Internet sites revealing their practices: see Wikipedia contributors, "Scientology versus the Internet," *Wikipedia, The Free Encyclopedia,* http://en .wikipedia.org/w/index.php?title=Scientology_versus_the_Internet&oldid=1 10441615. On keystroke software, see Janet Kornblum, "Prying Eyes are Everywhere," *USA Today Online,* posted April 13, 2005, http://www.usat oday.com/tech/news/2005-04-13-spyware_x.htm. On guest books, see Ian Urbina, "Sites Invite Online Mourning, but Don't Speak Ill of the Dead," *New York Times,* November 4, 2006. On wrestling, Ed Ferrara, a former World Wrestling Federation scriptwriter, told Wisconsin Public Radio's *To the Best of Our Knowledge* that it was the Internet that allowed the truth to be known: broadcast August 20, 2006; audio file available at http://www.wpr.org/ book/050605a.html. The Internet also made it possible for bookies to handle many more customers, "but it also made the average gambler, 'the square,' somewhat smarter too": see William Berlind, "Bookies in Exile," *New York Times Magazine*, August 17, 2003.

26. Frederick Levine, Christopher Locke, David (Doc) Searls, and David Weinberger*, The Cluetrain Manifesto: The End of Business as Usual* (Cambridge, MA: Perseus, 2000), 155.

27. William Gibson, "The Road to Oceania," *New York Times*, June 25, 2003, A27, also available through Web site of Global Business Network, http://www.gbn.org/ArticleDisplayServlet.srv?aid=7200.

28. On LAPD, see Alex Veiga, "Police Beating Video from L.A. Demonstrates the Power of YouTube—Again," *USA Today Online*, posted November 13, 2006, http://www.usatoday.com/tech/news/2006-11-13-youtube-arrest_x .htm?POE=TECISVA. On the New York City sanitation worker, see "Worker Caught Littering, Fining Storeowners," Web site of WABC TV, New York, posted October 23, 2006, http://abclocal.go.com/wabc/story?section=news &id=4688234.

29. J. D. Lasica, *Darknet: Hollywood's War against the Digital Generation* (Hoboken, NJ: John Wiley & Sons, 2005), 153.

30. Jonathan Finer, "The New Ernie Pyles: Sgtlizzie and 67cshdocs," *The Washington Post*, August 12, 2005, A01, http://www.washingtonpost.com/wp-dyn/content/article/2005/08/11/AR2005081102168.html; Martha Irvine, "Tell-all Blogs," *Capital Times* (Madison, WI), July 14 2005, 6E.

31. Daniel H. Pink, "Little Brother is Watching," *Wired*, July 2004, 25. On the impact of "inexpensive, lightweight cameras in the hands of private citizens, volunteer observers and the police themselves" on street protests, see Jim Dwyer, "Videos Challenge Accounts of Convention Unrest," *New York Times*, April 12, 2005, A1.

32. Katie Hafner and Saritha Rai, "Governments Tremble at Google's Bird's-Eye View," *New York Times*, December 20, 2005.

33. Katharine Q. Seelye, "Take That, Mr. Newsman," *New York Times*, January 2, 2006, C1.

34. Michiko Kakutani, "Bending the Truth in a Million Little Ways," Critic's Notebook, *New York Times*, January 17, 2006, B1. On the saga of "lonely-girl15," see Joshua Davis, "The Secret World of Lonelygirl," *Wired*, December 2006, 232. On false advertising, see Bruce Sterling, "The Sham Economy," *Wired*, March 2003, 78.

35. Davis, *TechGnosis*, 322.

36. On teenage blogs, see chap. 1, note 27 (Harmon). On teen-run pay-pornography sites, see Kurt Eichenwald, "Through His Webcam, a Boy Joins a Sordid Online World," *New York Times*, December 19, 2005, A1.

37. *Computer spam* is the unsolicited sending of bulk e-mails; *spyware* is hidden software that collects personal information about a user of a computer without the user's consent; a *computer virus* is a self-replicating program written to alter the way a computer operates, without the permission or knowledge of the user. Unlike a virus, a *computer worm* does not need to attach itself to an existing program, but does clog up network paths with unwanted traffic. One study, conducted by the Annenberg Public Policy Center, reported that almost three-quarters of the respondents couldn't understand what a Web site's privacy statement really meant, and that "half of American adult Internet users could not detect an illegal phishing e-mail message": see Tom Zeller, Jr., "You've Been Scammed Again, Maybe the Problem Isn't Your Computer," *New York Times*, June 6, 2005, C4. Almost 4,500 new viruses were created in the first half of 2004, compared to less than 1,000 for the corresponding period in 2003: see John Markoff, "Attacks on Windows PC's Grew in First Half of 2004," *New York Times*, September 20, 2004, C4; David Gallagher, "Users Find Too Many Phish in the Internet Sea," *New York Times*, September 20, 2004, C4. Examples of phishing are given at the "Report a Spoof" page on the Web site of Citigroup, http://www.citi.com/domain/spoof/reportspoof2.htm.

38. A *proxy server* allows users to access network services by going through a trusted filter, a computer that isolates the data source from the client requesting the information; a *firewall* is a program on a network router that only allows trusted external sites (IP addresses) to connect with its protected internal resources.

39. Seth Schiesel, "Growth of Wireless Internet Opens New Path for Thieves," *New York Times*, March 19, 2005.

40. For many, the perception of total interdependence instills the same kind of fear as infectious disease: see Davis, *TechGnosis*, 302.

41. "Persephone," "A Statue Turned its Head - a journal," a blog published at http://statue.iotoeuropa.org/index.php.

42. For a humorous take on life's filters, see Kate Zernike, "First, Your Water Was Filtered. Now It's Your Life," *New York Times,* March 21, 2004, WK4.

43. See chap. 5, note 27 (Gibson); Johnson, *Interface Culture,* 41.

44. This is the heart of the Shiboleth computer security schema being developed to allow students from different universities to access each other's libraries and course materials. It is also good practice for our human communications as well.

45. Andy Oram, "Peer-to-peer Offers an Opportunity to Rebuild the Foundations of the Internet," paper presented at Info-Tech2001, Osaka, Japan, November 15, 2001, http://www.praxagora.com/andyo/professional/p2p_foundation .html#security. Mr. Oram is a member of Computer Professionals for Social Responsibility. Used with permission.

46. Tim Gnatek, "Darknets: Virtual Parties With a Select Group of Invitees," *New York Times*, October 6, 2005, E2.

47. Bruce Schneier, "The Enemy Within," *Wired*, June 2003, http://www.wired .com/wired/archive/11.06/secure_spc.html; Jon Pareles, "The Court Ruled, So Enter The Geeks," *New York Times*, June 29, 2005, B1.

48. John Markoff, "By and for the Masses," *New York Times,* Business Day, June 29, 2005, C1.

49. Multiply Inc., "Multiply Introduces First Search Engine That Finds What's Been Published in Your Social Network," press release, *PR Newswire,* April 25, 2005. http://www.prnewswire.com/cgi-bin/stories.pl?ACCT=109& STORY=/www/story/04-25-2005/0003485044&EDATE. As is the case with most P2P systems, the problems of freeloading and trust are the most significant causes of error. One group of researchers has suggested that the answer is to create a subcategory of superpeers—those who stay connected for longer periods, are willing to share their recording preferences with others, and have

more "buddies" on their friends list. See Johan Pouwelse, Michiel van Slobbe, Jun Wang, Henk Sips, "P2P-based PVR Recommendations Using Friends, Taste Buddies and Superpeers," paper presented at 2005 International Conference on Intelligent User Interfaces, San Diego, CA, July 9–12, 2005, http://www.cs.vu.nl/ishare/public/I-Share-P6v1.0.pdf; session Web site at http://www.grouplens.org/beyond2005/papers.html.

50. For current examples of annotated maps, see ProgrammableWeb's site, http://www.programmableweb.com/api/GoogleMaps/mashups and *Wired*'s "Monkey Bites" blog, http://blog.wired.com/monkeybites/maps/index.html.

51. Michel Bauwens, "P2P and Human Evolution: Placing Peer to Peer Theory in an Integral Framework," draft paper shared with author on February 12, 2005; for a public draft, see http://integralvisioning.org/article.php?story=p2ptheory1.

52. eBay numbers from Kevin Kelly, "We Are the Web," *Wired*, August 2005, http://www.wired.com/wired/archive/13.08/tech.html.

53. Adam Liptak, "Criminal Records Erased by Courts Live to Tell Tales," *New York Times*, October 17, 2006.

54. David Shenk, "A Growing Web of Watchers Build A Surveillance Society," *New York Times*, Circuits Section, January 25, 2006, E6; Thomas Barnett, "Loving Big Brother," Scripps Howard News Service, November 19, 2006, http://www.shns.com/shns/g_index2.cfm?action=detail&pk=BARNETT-11-19-06.

55. Jeffrey Rosen, "Your Blog or Mine?" *New York Times Magazine*, December 19, 2004. YouTube was started in February 2005 with a few dozen videos; within ten months it had grown to a service with 35 million users watching 100 million clips each day. Google purchased it in October of 2006 for $1.65 billion. See Bob Garfield, "The YouTube Effect: You Tube vs. Boob Tube," *Wired*, December 2006, 222. After the killings at Virginia Tech in April of 2007, many social networkers saw "disconnection" at the root of the problem. See Virginia Heffernan, "Online, Students Say 'Reach Out to Loners,'" *New York Times*, April 19, 2007, E1.

56. As the *New York Times* reports, "young people can link to the profiles set up for these goods and services, . . . and these commercial 'friends' can even send them messages . . .": see Saul Hansell, "For MySpace, Making Friends Was Easy. Big Profit Is Tougher," *New York Times*, April 23, 2006. See also Saul Hansell, "Joining the Party, Eager to Make Friends," October 16, 2006, C1.

57. Alan Finder, "For Some, Online Persona Undermines a Resume," *New York Times*, June 11, 2006, A1.

58. Mark Buchanan, *Nexus: Small Worlds and the Groundbreaking Science of Networks* (New York: W. W. Norton, 2002), 45.

59. 2006 *MySpace* numbers from Wikipedia contributors, "MySpace," *Wikipedia, The Free Encyclopedia,* http://en.wikipedia.org/wiki/MySpace (accessed February 20, 2007). This *Wikipedia* entry estimates that by the first quarter of 2007, MySpace will have more than 150 million user accounts. "Users composed profiles for their pets . . . and household odds and ends (and then watched the conversation that developed between 'salt' and 'pepper')": see Michael Erard, "Decoding the New Cues in Online Society," *New York Times,* Circuits Section, November 27, 2003. On Amazon's "Real Names" problems, see "The Review of Reviews," *New York Times,* editorial, August 3, 2004, 18. On sex offenders with their own MySpace profiles, and how they were discovered using a "mash up" program that matched their names to the national database of registered sex offenders, see Kevin Poulsen, "MySpace Predator Caught by Code," *Wired News,* posted October 16, 2006, http://www.wired.com/news/technology/0,71948-0.html. On a new service to rent "friends" to mySpace subscribers, see Daniel E. Slotnik, "Too Few Friends? A Web Site Lets You Buy Some (and They're Hot)," *New York Times,* February 26, 2007, C4.

60. The *Times* reports on a national conference on "reputation mechanisms in online communities" held at the MIT Sloan School of Management: see Nicholas Thompson, "More Companies Pay Heed to their 'Word of Mouse' Reputation," *New York Times,* June 23, 2003, C4.

61. Chris Anderson, "The Long Tail," *Wired,* October 2004, 177.

62. Chris Anderson, *The Long Tail: Why the Future of Business is Selling More of Less* (New York: Hyperion, 2006), chap. 7.

63. According to Kelly, "One study found that only 40 percent of the Web is commercial. The rest runs on duty or passion": chap. 5, note 52. The "sharing economy" has become a new economic force in the digitally networked P2P environment: see David Kirpatrick, "Money Makes the World Go Round—or Does It?" *Fortune Online,* July 25, 2005, http://www.fortune.com/fortune/fastforward/0,15704,1088315,00.html (page now discontinued); article summarized at http://technology360.typepad.com/technology360/2005/07/money_makes_the.html. Yochai Benkler, a law professor and economist at Yale, has attempted to precisely describe these cooperative volunteer projects in several papers offered at his Web site, http://www.benkler.org/Pub.html#Commons. Of course, the market side is far from banished. Even video-game communities are replete with "farmers" interested in selling—for real dollars—the virtual currency that allows gamers to buy swords, armor, and other tools of battle: see Seth Schiesel, "Virtual Achievement for Hire: It's Only Wrong If You Get Caught," *New York Times,* December 9, 2005, C4.

64. Kevin McGee and Jörgen Skågeby, "Gifting Technologies," *First Monday, Special Issue: Music and the Internet,* July 2005, http://www.firstmonday.org/issues/issue9_12/mcgee/index.html. Links in original. Used with permission.

65. Lisa Guernsey, "In the Lecture Hall, a Geek Chorus," *New York Times,* July 24, 2003, E1.

66. Michel Bauwens, "Peer to Peer: From Technology to Politics to a New Civilisation?" posted on the Integration Web site, http://noosphere.cc/peer ToPeer.html (site now discontinued; archived at http://zweite.oekonux-kon ferenz.de/dokumentation/texte/Bauwens.html and http://www.oekonux. org/list-en/archive/msg01089.html). Bauwens cites Jorge N. Ferrer, *Revisioning Transpersonal Theory: A Participatory Vision of Human Spirituality* (Albany: SUNY Press, 2001). John Heron's *Participatory Spirituality: A Farewell to Authoritarian Religion* (Morrisville, NC: Lulu Press, 2006) expands on this idea. Or, in another tradition, "As Murshid Moineddin [Jablonsky, late Head of the Sufi Ruhaniat Order] wrote...'I am not Murshid; we are Murshid. I do not have all the answers; we may have the answers'": see Samuel L. Lewis and Neil Douglas-Klotz, "The Sacred Circle" *Toward the One: A Journal of Unity* 7 (Spring 2006), 20, http://www.sufi movement.org/pdf/TTO_2006.pdf.

67. Malcolm Gladwell, "The Cellular Church," *New Yorker*, September 12, 2005, 60.

68. Al-Qaeda and its offshoots have created Web sites for sharing terror tactics, including recipes for ricin poison and diagrams of various antipersonnel weapons. See Steve Coll and Susan B. Glasser, "Few Obstacles Deter Cyberterrorists," *Washington Post*, August 9, 2005, referenced at *Boston Globe* online site, http://www.boston.com/news/world/articles/2005/08/09/few _obstacles_deter_cyber_terrorists/. Howard Bloom's comment is from an interview on *All in the Mind* ABC Radio National (Australia), November 10, 2002, http://www.abc.net.au/rn/science/mind/s719643.htm. On the isolating and group-reinforcing power of online chat rooms, see Nadya Labi, "Jihad 2.0," *Atlantic Monthly*, July/August 2006, 102, and David Samuels, "Let's Die Together," *Atlantic Monthly*, May 2007, 92.

69. On public distrust of journalism, see Nicholas Kristof, "A Slap in the Face," op-ed column, *New York Times,* April 12, 2005, A23. The good news for public television stations is that even as they are losing funding and viewers to cable and the Internet, the public considers them a "sanctuary of trustworthiness": see "PBS Number One in Public Trust According to New Roper Poll," Web site of PBS*,* August 4, 2004, http://www.pbs.org/aboutpbs/news/ 20040205_RoperPollRelease.html. For fears of White House interference in public TV, see Stephen Labaton, Lorne Manly, and Elizabeth Jensen, "Republican Chairman Exerts Pressure on PBS, Alleging Biases," *New York Times*, May 2, 2005, A1. For discussion of television's "parasitic" metainformation shows, see Johnson, *Interface Culture*, 36.

70. Johnson, *Everything Bad Is Good for You*, 99; Steven Johnson, "Watching TV Makes You Smarter," *New York Times Magazine*, April 25, 2005.

71. Johnson, "Watching TV Makes You Smarter," chap. 5, note 70.

72. Jesse Hamlin, "Gore's New Media Venture Seeks to Blend TV, Internet" *San Francisco Chronicle,* April 5, 2005, http://sfgate.com/cgi-bin/article.cgi?file=/c/a/2005/04/05/GORE.TMP. On viewer ads, see Julie Bosman, "An Agency's Worst Nightmare: Ads Created by Users," *New York Times,* May 11, 2006. Current's Web site is http://www.current.tv.

73. Frank Rich, "Yes, You Are the Person of the Year!" *New York Times*, op-ed column, December 24, 2006, http://select.nytimes.com/2006/12/24/opinion/24rich.html?hp.

74. Sufi master Hazrat Inayat Khan likens this process to a traveler who absent-mindedly tosses some old seeds on the ground and walks on, not knowing that the earth, sun, water, and air will bring them to fruitfulness long after he is gone: see Inayat Khan, *The Heart of Sufism: Essential Writings* (Boston: Shambhala, 1999), 139.

75. Blanton, *Radical Honesty,* 57.

76. Wauters, *Chakras and Their Archetypes,* 119.

77. "Personal awareness is largely this stream of roof-brain talk. Even when actual feedback from another source is coming in, roof-brain chatter goes right ahead, prestructuring, tape-looping, resenting, planning one's rebuttal, fogging inputs and creating static": see Joseph Chilton Pearce, *Exploring the Crack in the Cosmic Egg* (New York: Julian Press, 1974), 82.

78. Sri Aurobindo cited in White, *The Meeting of Science and Spirit*, 96.

79. For a discussion of "small networks" see Buchanan, *Nexus.*

SIXTH-LEVEL

1. Laszlo, *Science and the Akashic Field,* 140; Wilber interview, see chap. 5, note 1; Wilber, *A Theory of Everything,* n. 114. Neuroscience is discovering that the brain has its own receptors for "seeing deeper." For example, the release of the neurotransmitter anandamide (triggered by drugs such as marijuana and by chanting, meditation, and religious bliss) has the effect of slowing the processing of peripheral data, allowing one to dive fully into the "now" of the moment and the purity of the object (or in Buddhism, the "nonobject") of contemplation. See Michael Pollan, *The Botany of Desire: A Plant's Eye View of the World* (New York: Random House, 2001), 147–168.

2. Satprem, *Sri Aurobindo,* 168, 66; Judith, *Waking the Global Heart,* 214 (chart).

3. Judith, *Eastern Body Western Mind,* 358; Anodea Judith and Selene Vega, *The*

Sevenfold Journey: Reclaiming Mind, Body and Spirit through the Chakras (Freedom, CA: The Crossing Press, 1993), 225; Wauters, *Chakras and Their Archetypes*, 137; Fox, *Sins of the Spirit*, 301. Beck and Cowan (*Spiral Dynamics*, 277) call this state "peak Yellow" moving towards Turquoise.

4. On *Dharmadatu*, see Yutang Lin, "Dharmadatu," August 17, 2001, http://www.angelfire.com/realm/bodhisattva/dharmadhatu.html. Dr. Lin is the main disciple of the late Yogi C. M. Chen (1906–1987). His study center (online at http://www.yogichen.org/intro_e.html) is located in El Cerrito California. The full line from Blake is "To see a World in a Grain of Sand / And a Heaven in a Wild Flower / Hold Infinity in the palm of your hand / And Eternity in an hour": see William Blake, "Augeries of Innocence" (1803), http://www.poetryloverspage.com/poets/blake/to_see_world.html.

5. This focus on the "essence" of the mundane is discussed in Pollan, *Botany of Desire*, 147; Wilber, *A Theory of Everything*, 60; and Laszlo, *Science and the Akashic Field*, 141.

6. On multimedia and "seeing beyond *maya*," see Introduction, note 8 (Davidson). Douglas-Klotz, *Sufi Book of Life*, 100.

7. Poem from Douglas-Klotz, *Sufi Book of Life*, 219. Used by permission of Penguin, a division of Penguin Group (USA) Inc.

8. Wilber, *The Atman Project*, 154.

9. Paul Verhoeven, director of *Total Recall* (a 1990 film based on a Philip K. Dick short story), quoted in Frank Rose, "The Second Coming of Philip K. Dick," *Wired,* December 2003. Dick was also the author of the short stories adapted for the films *Blade Runner* (1982) and *Minority Report* (2002).

10. *Al-Basir!*—one of the "99 Names of God" in the Muslim tradition: see Douglas-Klotz, *Sufi Book of Life*, 72.

11. This "creative" process is of course perfectly acceptable with home movies and snapshots, but not in science. Some professional journals have discovered "enhanced" illustrations in research manuscripts. In a few fraudulent cases, new elements were added or conflicting images removed. See Nicholas Wade, "It May Look Authentic; Here's How to Tell It Isn't," *New York Times*, January 24, 2006, D1.

12. Elvis Mitchell calls Martin Scorsese's comments on the Criterion Collection's laser disk of the film *Taxi Driver* more than a commentary: "[It] isn't just an interview; it's a master class, with an intoxicating wealth of raw data and insight into his perspective." See Elvis Mitchell, "Everyone's a Film Geek Now," *New York Times*, Arts and Leisure Section, August 17, 2003, AR1.

13. The high-definition image does not require the same level of image-completion as analog TV. Its impact is not at the fourth chakra but is more about fifth-

level issues of truth-telling and sixth-level understanding of the importance of decoding. HD's "harder" image has apparently created problems with the video pornography industry. Viewer fantasies have collided with HD's super-high resolution, which reveals every blemish and stretch mark on the idealized sex object. See Matt Richtel, "In Raw World of Sex Movies, High Definition Could Be a View Too Real," *New York Times,* January 22, 2007, C1.

14. Nick Paumgarten, "Bad-Ass Camera," *New Yorker,* August 21, 2006, 26.

15. Because only a fraction of the power is found on any single frequency, it is difficult to detect, and jamming one frequency won't affect the rest of the transmission. For a discussion of the new uses for spread-spectrum, see Jesse Sunerblick, "Into the Great Wide Open," *Columbia Journalism Review*, March/April 2005, http://www.cjr.org/issues/2005/2/sunenblick.asp.

16. Spread-spectrum's ability to resist enemy interception and jamming made it a perfect candidate for military communications. Lamarr didn't use her stage name on the patent, and it never made her any money. See "What is Digital Spread Spectrum As Used in Cordless Telephones?" HowStuffWorks Web site, http://electronics.howstuffworks.com/question326.htm. According to writer Tim Barkow, "Hedy's own discovery of spread spectrum probably began after eavesdropping on conversations between her ex-husband, Austrian munitions magnate Fritz Mandl, and his colleagues at their Vienna home, where the young actress lived during the early 1930s before fleeing her oppressive husband and his Nazi pals for England and then Hollywood." For more of his version of the story, see Tim Barkow, "Delilah and the Bad Boy," posted February 11, 2004, at his Web site, http://thinkcorps.com/2004/02/11/delilah-and-the-bad-boy/.

17. Susan Blackmore, *The Meme Machine* (New York: Oxford, 1999), 213. A synopsis of the book is at Blackmore's Web site, http://www.susan blackmore.co.uk/Books/Meme%20Machine/mmsynop. html.

18. Michael Talbot, *The Holographic Universe* (New York: HarperCollins, 1991), 27. In *The Field* (New York: HarperCollins, 2002), Lynn McTaggart cites the work of Karl Pribram to build a mathematical model of perception based upon Fourier transformations, the same "cosine quantization" tools used in today's video compression standards. See also Peter Russell, *The Global Brain* (Los Angeles: Tarcher, 1983). Loosely speaking, the Fourier transform decomposes an analog function into a continuous spectrum of its frequency components.

19. Bloom, *The Global Brain*, 66.

20. Blackmore, *Meme Machine*, 216.

21. Robert X. Cringely, "TV Oaxaca: How Narrowband Streaming Video Could Serve 90 Million Stranded Americans," "I, Cringely" Web site, weekly column posted July 1, 2004, http://www.pbs.org/cringely/pulpit/2004/pulit_20040701

_000817.html. On "prewiring" to recognize sexual images and celebrities, see Diane Martindale, "One Face, One Neuron," *Scientific American*, October 2, 2005, http://www.sciam.com/article.cfm?articleID=00087A9B-A742 -1330-A54583414B7F0000.

22. According to an entry in *Wikipedia*, "in actual fact, no such research was carried out at Cambridge University. It all started with a letter to the *New Scientist* magazine from Graham Rawlinson in which he discusses his Ph.D. thesis: *In a puiltacibon of New Scnieitst you could ramdinose all the letetrs, keipeng the first two and last two the same, and reibadailty would hadrly be aftcfeed* [sic]," Wikipedia contributors, "Typoglycemia," *Wikipedia, The Free Encyclopedia*, http://en.wikipedia.org/w/index.php?title=Typoglycemia&old id=108845724 (accessed February 19, 2007).

23. Grossinger, *Integration of Nature*, 190.

24. In fact, your experience of "reality" is always a half-second behind: that's the latency time your inner decoder takes to process and produce its facsimile of "truth" in visual awareness. For a brief discussion of "back-dating" reality, see Paul Grobstein, "Timing The Conscious and the Unconscious: Some Implications for Thinking . . . and Thinking About Time," on the Web site of the Center for Science in Society, Bryn Mawr College, March 18, 2003, http://serendip.brynmawr.edu/local/scisoc/time/time.html. See also Rita Carter, *Consciousness* (London: Weidenfeld and Nicolson, an imprint of Orion Books, 2003).

25. The "selfplex," she argues, has evolved to support our role as communicating beings, spreading bits of ideas—memes—into the Infosphere. "The selfplex is successful not because it is true or good or beautiful; not because it helps our genes; nor because it makes us happy. It is successful because the memes that get inside it persuade us to work for their propagation": see Blackmore, *Meme Machine*, 234.

26. Compiled from Mark Long, "Understanding MPEG-2 Digital Video Compression," at http://www.mlesat.com/Article7.html (site now restricted); Dr. Ivan B. Tonklemousse, "Understanding MPEG-2 Compression," Web site of Creative Video Productions, September 19, 2005, http://www.creative video.co.uk/public/articles.php?article=8; and Wikipedia contributors, "Video Compression Picture Types," *Wikipedia, The Free Encyclopedia*, http://en.wikipedia.org/w/index.php?title=Video_compression_picture_types &oldid=100117900.

27. Davis, *TechGnosis*, 181. That is, unless they've been posted on the Internet! See chap. 5, note 25.

28. Frank Rose, "The Second Coming of Philip K. Dick," *Wired*, December 2003; Edward Rothstein, "Pursuing the 17th-Century Origins of the Hacker's

Grail," *New York Times*, September 20, 2003, A17. See also Davis, *TechGnosis*, 273–4.

29. Examples include "ambient" ads projected on sidewalks and building walls; "stealth" ads include everything from unacknowledged "product placements" in movies and TV shows and the hiring of actors to go into public places and tout their attachment to specific brands, to the recent hiding of flashing cartoon images on Boston highways. "Virtual" ads are created by using computer imaging technology to add products to TV or movie scenes that were never there to begin with. See "Advertising: It's Everywhere," summary on the Web site of Media Awareness Network, http://www.media-awareness.ca/english/parents/marketing/advertising_everywhere.cfm.

30. Jonathan Wilson, "Intro to Seduction," review of *Reunion* by Alan Lightman, *New York Times Book Review*, July 27, 2003, 6.

31. Thompson, *Coming Into Being*, 194.

32. Video-game sales for the month of November 2006 totaled $1.7 billion, up thirty-four percent year-over-year. U.S. software sales climbed fifteen percent to $804 million. Data from James Brightman, "Breaking: November Game Industry Sales Skyrocket 34%," *Game Daily*, posted December 7, 2006, http://biz.gamedaily.com/industry/feature/?id=14685.

33. Clive Thompson, "Saving The World, One Video Game at a Time," *New York Times*, section 2, July 23, 2006, 1; United Nations, "Saving Lives 'Cool' As Humanitarian Video Game Surpasses One Million Players," press release, World Food Programme, May 31, 2005, http://www.food-force.com/downloads/one-million-players.doc. The game itself can be found at http://www.food-force.com/.

34. Johnson, *Everything Bad Is Good for You*, 37.

35. J. D. Lasica (in *Darknet*, 244) describes *Second Life* as a game that lets people express their personalities and display their creativity in "a rich, diverse landscape filled with interesting characters, whimsical domains, and cool getaways." See also Kevin Maney's profile of *Second Life* creator Philip Rosedale in *USA Today*, February 5, 2007, 1B. On *Second Life's* environmental activists, see Lisa Selin Davis, "Click Here to Create a Better World," *onearth* (Natural Resources Defense Council), Spring 2007.

36. On the psychological space of multiplayer game domains, see Wertheim, *Pearly Gates of Cyberspace*, 235–52, and David Williamson Shaffer, Kurt R. Squire, Richard Halverson, and James P. Gee, "Videogames and the Future of Learning," Academic Advanced Distributed Learning Co-Laboratory, University of Wisconsin-Madison, December 10, 2004, http://www.academiccolab.org/resources/gappspaper1.pdf. The decision in late 2005 to "revamp" the popular online multiplayer simulation game *Star Wars Galaxies* into more

of a shoot-em-up experience (to attract younger players) left most of its 200,000 adult participants in great despair over the loss of both relationships and communities that they might have spent many hundreds of hours constructing. See Seth Schiesel, "For Online Star Wars Game, It's Revenge of the Fans," *New York Times*, December 10, 2005, C1. On the future of games, see Jonathan Rauch, "Sex, Lies, and Videogames," *Atlantic Monthly*, November 2006, 76. On games as an art form, see for example, Henry Jenkins, "Art Form for the Digital Age," *Technology Review*, September/October 2000, http://www.technologyreview.com/read_article.aspx?id=12189&ch=infotech.

37. Mark Carreau, "NASA to Send Shuttle to Repair the Hubble Space Telescope," *Houston Chronicle* Web site, October 31, 2006, http://www.chron.com/disp/story.mpl/space/4299052.html. Patrick Di Justo reports on the number of unmonitored Webcams, including those found in a middle school locker room, that can be accessed with a simple Google search: see "On the Net, Unseen Eyes," *New York Times*, Circuits Section, February 24, 2005, E136.

38. Steven Johnson, "The Long Zoom," *New York Times Magazine*, October 8, 2006, 50. On disruptions to ways of "seeing" space, see Wertheim, *Pearly Gates of Cyberspace*, and Shlain, *Art and Physics*.

39. In the Vedic scriptures, the world of maya is believed to be an illusion, a veiling of the true unitary nature of the cosmos. On changing "operating systems," see Judith and Vega, *Sevenfold Journey*, 226.

40. This story has been told and retold in many traditions. Rumi tells it in his poem, "The Elephant in the Dark" from *Tales from Masnavi*. A summary can be found in Wikipedia contributors, "Blind Men and an Elephant," *Wikipedia, The Free Encyclopedia*, http://en.wikipedia.org/w/index.php?title=Blind_Men_and_an_Elephant&oldid=106612276.

41. Pollan (*Botany of Desire*, 170) describes the brain chemistry of transcendence. Physicist Amit Goswami argues that once the brain's habitual decoding buffer is cleared, we have a new choice, whether to let our ego-identity act on external stimuli, or in the gap between receiving incoming data and deciding to "decode" it, we can make the "quantum leap" necessary to transform our inner consciousness: see Goswami, *Self-Aware Universe*, 234.

42. Wauters, *Chakras and Their Archetypes*, 138.

43. Douglas-Klotz, *Sufi Book of Life*, 92, 226.

44. Klotz (chap. 4, note 30). On a Sufi interpretation of *at-Tawwâb*, see Richard Shelquist (Wahiduddin), "*at-Tawwâb*," http://wahiduddin.net/words/99_pages/tawwab_80.htm. Our true face is in Buddhism called "Original Mind": see Stephen Levine, *Turning Toward the Mystery* (New York: HarperCollins, 2002), 57.

45. Rig Veda, I.164.20, cited in Satprem, *Sri Aurobindo*, 44.

46. On pulling out to larger field, see Goswami, *Self-Aware Universe*, 237; Satprem, *Sri Aurobindo*, 50.

47. On "inter-being," see Thich Nhat Hanh, *The Heart of Understanding: Commentaries on the Prajnaparamita Heart Sutra* (Berkeley: Parallax Press, 1988), excerpt on Parallax Press Web site at http://www.parallax.org/cgi-bin/shopper.cgi?preadd=action&key=BOOKHOU.

48. Vilayat Inayat Khan, *Toward the One* (New York: Harper Colophon, 1974), 155, 159. Khan warns that at death "you will be removed to whatever plane corresponds to your aspirations." His suggestion: Aspire for the highest plane.

49. Replacing dark rays of suffering with light is at the heart of the Buddhist "Tonglen" breathing meditation. See Thrangu Rinpoche, "Tonglen—'Sending and Taking,'" record of oral teachings given December 1993, posted at the Quiet Mountain, Inc., gateway Web site, http://www.quietmountain.org/links/teachings/tonglen.htm, and Pema Chödrön, "Tonglen Meditation: Changing Pain into Compassion," transcript of excerpts from the audiotape *Good Medicine* (Boulder, CO: Sounds True, 2001), posted at the Web site of Beliefnet, http://www.beliefnet.com/story/4/story_425_1.html.

50. "Installing Love," published on the Web site of HumanHealing.com, http://www.humanhealing.com/stories/installing-love.php.

51. The first mantra is pronounced *Gatay, Gatay, para Gatay, para sum Gatay, Bodhi Svaha*. This has been call the "mantra of all mantras," the mantra that dissipates the pain of the ego-self, connecting the practitioner with the truth that nothing is really separate from the Divine. The Hindu "*neti-neti*" practice is also a way of remembering that we can never really know the true nature of God; rather, all we can say is "It is not this, nor this." Kabbalah comes to the same understanding, calling God *Ein Sof*, "there is no end."

SEVENTH-LEVEL

1. On "quantum mind" see Goswami (1993), 225. Ervin Laszlo (*Science and the Akashic Field*, 105) calls this the A-Field, saying that the "information field that links quanta and galaxies in the physical universe and cells and organisms in the biosphere also links the brains and minds of humans in the sociosphere." On the Beloved, see Douglas-Klotz, *Sufi Book of Life*, 130.

2. Expressed as the (Turquoise) "holistic meme" of Spiral Dynamics: see Beck and Cowan, *Spiral Dynamics*, 47, 289.

3. Wilber, *The Spectrum of Consciousness*, 287–88; Judith, *Waking the Global Heart*, 253.

4. He continues, "There isn't a real distinction between . . . a crop circle and a technological breakthrough transmitted in a dream, the Seth material and the Course in Miracles. Information is trying to get through any way it can . . .": see Grossinger, *Integration of Nature*, 195.

5. In Carl Jung's term, our "collective unconscious." This database holds all the information ever available to human consciousness. Mystical seventh-level awareness can tap into this repository to "know" virtually anything. This is the domain of the shaman and the spiritual healer who can access the "the etheric template" and change its codes.

6. Satprem, *Sri Aurobindo*, 66.

7. Ibid., 268.

8. On sound at the seventh level, see Kahn, *Toward the One*, 201.

9. Mosco, *The Digital Sublime*, 21.

10. Jim Banister, *Word of Mouse: The New Age of Networked Media* (Chicago: Agate, 2004), 114.

11. See "Grid Computing: SETI@home, The Proof That It Works," at the Web site of Grid.org, http://www.grid.org/about/gc/seti.htm. For a current list of grid projects see Wikipedia contributors, "List of Distributed Computing Projects," *Wikipedia, The Free Encyclopedia,* http://en.wikipedia.org/w/index.php?title=List_of_distributed_computing_projects&oldid=108378221.

12. For Jinni (Java INference engine and Networked Interactor), see Paul Tarau, "Inference and Computation Mobility with Jinni," posted at Tarau's Web site at the Department of Computer Science and Engineering, University of North Texas, March 23, 1999, http://logic.csci.unt.edu/tarau/research/NewJinni Papers/jpaper.html. On Ajax, see Jesse Garrett, "Ajax: A New Approach to Web Applications," posted at the Web site of Adaptive Path, February 18, 2005, http://www.adaptivepath.com/publications/essays/archives/000385.php. See also John Markoff, "The Time Is Now: Bust Up The Box!" *New York Times*, Circuits Section, October 6, 2005, E1. In addition to computing cycles and software sharing, the grid has made possible the creation of entirely new applications based on the "mashing up" of programs running on different servers in different places, tapping intelligence stored at multiple locations. Some of the most popular involve linking Google maps to other databases, generating everything from maps of apartments advertised on craigslist, New York City parking garages, and the birth cities of every Oscar winner. A current list of mashed-up Google maps is available at http://www.googlemaps mania.blogspot.com.

13. Anderson, *The Long Tail.*

14. Brad Stone, "For DVDs, the Future is Gloomy," *New York Times*, November 29, 2006, C1; John Markoff, "Software Out There: Programming a Revolution Piecemeal," *New York Times*, April 5, 2006, E1. The BBC experiment is described at the Web site of the Creative Archive License Group, http://www.bbc.co.uk/calc/news/ and is also cited by Lasica, *Darknet*, 181. On the global library, see Kevin Kelly, "Scan this Book!" *New York Times Magazine*, May 14, 2006, 43.

15. On arts-based mash-ups, see "You Say Mashup, I Say Mash-up," posted at the Web site of Mashup.com, http://www.mashup.com/about.htm. An interesting remix example is Francis Shanahan's virtual photocollage site. She takes images from the Web that match up with the interests of her subjects and then aligns them to form a collage portrait of that person. She has created portraits of Jeff Bezos using 8,000 space and science-related product images, of Clint Eastwood using 4,275 *Sesame Street* images, and of Julia Roberts using 3,000 beauty product images: see http://www.francisshanahan.com/detail.aspx?cid=353.

16. Kate Zernike, "Tired of TiVo? Beyond Blogs? Podcasts are Here and Multiplying," *New York Times,* February 19, 2005, 1; Steven Humphries, "Podcasts meld MP3 players, RSS in Radio Fashion," *USA Today*, Tech Products, posted December 10, 2004, http://www.usatoday.com/tech/products/services/2004-12-10-podcasts_x.htm; Matthew Fordahl, "'Podcasting' Lets Masses Do Radio Shows," *USA Today* (Associated Press), posted February 7, 2005, http://www.usatoday.com/tech/news/2005-02-07-podcasting_x.htm?csp=34. A creator of Web content creates a standardized RSS form that is then posted to an RSS distributor. Users subscribe to specific RSS updates that tell their Web browsers to go to a specific URL and download the new materials.

17. Scott McNealy, "A Letter from Scott McNealy," published as part of "The Participation Age," a conference held at the United Nations June 6, 2005, and posted at the Web site of Sun Microsystems, http://www.sun.com/about sun/media/features/participate-un.html.

18. John Markoff, "H. P. to Unveil Radio Chips to Store Data," *New York Times,* July 17, 2006, C8.

19. Jerry Kang and Dana Cuff, "Pervasive Computing: Embedding the Public Sphere," *Washington and Lee Law Review* 62, no. 1 (Winter 2005), 93–146, abstract at http://papers.ssrn.com/sol3/papers.cfm?abstract_id=626961.

20. See chap. 5, note 54 (Barnett).

21. "Wisdom reputation" quote from Shumpei Kumon, President of the Global Communications Institute in Tokyo, cited in Howard Rheingold, *The Virtual Community: Homesteading on the Electronic Frontier* (Reading, MA: Addison-

Wesley, 1993), chap. 7, http://www.rheingold.com/vc/book/7.html. See also chap. 5, note 66 (Bauwens). The importance of recognizing hierarchies of knowledge is stressed by Chris Cowen in response to Bauwen's optimistic view of P2P. Cowan warns that "flat egalitarianism" leaves too much room for community-destroying "fools, fast-talkers and saboteurs": see Chris Cowen, "Is P2P for everybody?" posted in a weblog hosted at the Web site of the P2P Foundation, April 22, 2006, http://blog.p2pfoundation.net/is-p2p-for-every-body/2006/04/22.

22. Scott Kirsner, "Smart Dust," *Fast Company,* December 2003, 93.

23. Steve Lohr, "Digital (Fill in the Blanks) Is on the Horizon," *New York Times,* August 1, 2003, A1. On the toaster, see Andrew Orlowski, "Java Toaster Prints Weather Forecast," *The Register* (UK), March 30, 2001, http://www.theregis ter.co.uk/2001/03/30/java_toaster_prints_weather_forecast/. On Ambient Devices' products, see http://www.ambientdevices.com/cat/products.html; its customers, both happy and unhappy, share their thoughts at http://www .ambient411.com/.

24. "Stoves will conspire with the refrigerators to decide what recipe makes the best use of the available ingredients, then guide us through preparation of the recipe with the aid of a network-connected food processor and blender. Or they will communicate to optimize the energy usage in our households": see "Pervasive Computing," Web site of the Bombay Section of the Institute of Electrical and Electronic Engineers, Inc., http://www.ewh.ieee.org/r10/bom bay/news4/Pervasive_Computing.htm.

25. GE Consumer & Industrial, "What's For Dinner? Just Call Your Refrigera-tor," press release, http://www.geconsumerproducts.com/pressroom/press_ releases/company/company/kitchenoffuture_article_06.htm.

26. "If we take one step towards God, God takes ten steps towards us; if we walk towards Him, He will run towards us!" This is a *hadith* (saying, beatitude) attributed to the Prophet.

27. Fox, *Sins of the Spirit,* 112.

28. Ervin Laszlo (*Science and the Akashic Field,* 57) describes this "akashic field" as an extrasomatic unlimited capacity database of all memory.

29. Aurobindo, *The Future Evolution of Man: The Divine Life Upon Earth,* ed. P. G. Saint-Hilaire (Pondicherry, India: All India Press, 1963), chap. 6.

30. On Hollywood's war against the freedom of the Internet, see Lasica, *Darknet.*

31. Hershock, *Reinventing the Wheel.*

32. Goswami (*Self-Aware Universe,* 225) believes that our nonlocal consciousness can tap the content of the global brain, "pure mental states that extend far beyond the local experiences within the lifetime of one person." Vilayat Inayat

Khan (Inayat's son) described the process of *wazaif* meditation on the divine names and attributes of God as "drawing from the Divine Treasury" in order to be of service to the Universe: see Vilayat Inayat Khan, *Awakening: A Sufi Experience* (New York: Jeremy P. Tarcher, 1999), 24.

33. Satprem, *Sri Aurobindo*, 288.

34. Michel Bauwens, "The 'Great Cosmic Mash-up' As an Answer to Postmodernist Fragmentation," posted in a weblog hosted at the Web site of the P2P Foundation, February 26, 2006, http://blog.p2pfoundation.net/the-mash-up-era-as-an-answer-to-postmodernist-fragmentation/2006/02/26.

35. "Blinkenlights" photos and a description of the project are at http://www.blinkenlights.de/.

36. Jessie Scanlon, "If Walls Could Talk, Streets Might Join In," *New York Times*, Circuits Section, September 18, 2003, E7. A number of libraries have created "Community Mirrors" that project in real time what patrons are searching for. This visualization is displayed on a large screen projection in the entrance area of the library and optionally on mobile devices. See Michael Koch, "Building Community Mirrors with Public Shared Displays," Proceedings of eChallenges 2004, Vienna, Austria, October 2004, available at Koch's Web site at Technische Universität München, http://www11.informatik.tu-muenchen.de/publications/pdf/Koch2004a.pdf.

37. For Sky Ear, see the event's Web site, http://www.haque.co.uk/skyear.

38. See design examples from Open Doors: The Design Challenge of Pervasive Computing, session held November 15, 2002, at conference Doors of Perception 7: Flow, Amsterdam, November 14–16, 2002, http://flow.doorsofperception.com/opendoorsprojects.html.

39. Aurobindo, *Future Evolution of Man*, 125.

40. For more on the *Umbrella.net* project, see http://www.spectropolis.info/umbrella.php.

41. Jim Banister uses a core seventh-level metaphor when he describes grid computing as taking a piece of consciousness and putting it into the universal field: It would be as if you were able to take a math problem occupying your brain, or a large chunk of your childhood memories, and break them down into individually unrecognizable fragments in order to distribute them throughout the brains of thousands or millions of your fellow humans, who might be better suited to handle that math problem, or who might have unused memory capacity. See Banister, *Word of Mouse*, 114. On the programmable nanochips, see John Markoff, chap. 7, note 18.

42. On Rumi's flute, see Inayat Khan, *The Sufi Message*, Vol. 5, *In an Eastern Rose Garden*, 2nd ed. (Geneva: International Sufi Movement, 1979), 137. On

tikkun, see Daniel C. Matt, *God and the Big Bang* (Woodstock, VT: Jewish Lights, 1996), 86–89.

43. Khan, *The Sufi Message*, 136.

44. Ibid., 194.

45. Judith, *Waking the Global Heart*, 319. On the Web as making explicit the ongoing process of the fluidity of self, see Wertheim, *Pearly Gates of Cyberspace*, 251.

46. On angels, see Khan, *Heart of Sufism*, 110.

47. Pir Vilayat Inayat Khan describes these "seed program" tools as "the 'mantram' of the Hindus, the 'nembutsu' of the Buddhists, the repetitions of *Kyrie Eleison* of the Hesychasts, Orthodox hermit monks, [or] the '*wazifa*' of the Sufis." See Vilayat Inayat Khan, *Toward the One*, 202. Hazrat's grandson (and Vilayat's son) Pir Zia, has described the four stages of *zikr* sound practices in a PBS interview. In the final stage of this practice, the mind keeps the seed sound going silently within, even when the outer consciousness is engaged fully in day-to-day life. See Pir Zia Khan, interview, *Religion & Ethics Newsweekly*, PBS, episode 610, November 8, 2002, transcript at http://www.pbs.org/wnet/religionandethics/week610/pir.html.

48. Offered by Anodea Judith to the author, November 6, 2006

Selected Bibliography

Anderson, Chris. *The Long Tail: Why the Future of Business Is Selling Less of More.* New York: Hyperion, 2006.

Aurobindo (Ghose). *The Future Evolution of Man: The Divine Life Upon Earth.* 2nd ed. Edited by P. B. Saint-Hilaire. Pondicherry, India: All India Press, 1963.

Banister, Jim. *Word of Mouse: The New Age of Networked Media.* Chicago: Agate, 2004.

Barnouw, Erik. *The Golden Web: A History of Broadcasting in the United States 1933–1953.* New York, Oxford University Press, 1968.

———. *A Tower in Babel: A History of Broadcasting in the United States to 1933.* New York: Oxford University Press, 1966.

Beck, Don, and Christopher Cowan. *Spiral Dynamics: Mastering Values, Leadership and Change.* Oxford: Blackwell, 1996.

Becker, Ernst. *Escape from Evil.* New York: The Free Press, 1975.

Blackmore, Susan. *The Meme Machine.* New York: Oxford, 1999.

Blanton, Brad. *Radical Honesty.* New York: Dell Trade Paperback, 1996.

Bloom, Howard. *The Global Brain: The Evolution of Mass Mind from the Big Bang to the 21st Century.* New York: Wiley, 2000.

Bryson, Bill. *A Short History of Nearly Everything.* New York: Broadway Books, 2003.

Buchanan, Mark. *Nexus: Small Worlds and the Groundbreaking Science of Networks.* New York: W. W. Norton, 2002.

Carter, Rita. *Consciousness.* London: Weidenfeld and Nicolson, an imprint of Orion Books, 2003.

Cheney, Margaret. *Tesla: Man Out of Time.* New York: Dorset Press, 1981.

Cobb, Jennifer. *Cybergrace: The Search for God in the Digital World.* New York: Crown, 1998.

Cohen, Norman J. *Hineini in Our Lives: Learning How to Respond to Others through Fourteen Biblical Texts and Personal Stories.* Woodstock, VT: Jewish Lights, 2004.

Czitrom, Daniel J. *Media and the American Mind: From Morse to McLuhan.* Chapel Hill: University of North Carolina Press, 1982.

Dark, David. *Everyday Apocalypse.* Grand Rapids, MI: Brazos Press, 2002.

Davidson, Randall. *9XM Talking: WHA Radio and the Wisconsin Idea.* Madison: University of Wisconsin Press, 2006.

Davis, Erik. *TechGnosis: Myth, Magic and Mysticism in the Age of Information.* New York: Harmony Books, 1998.

de Quincey, Christian. *Radical Nature: Rediscovering the Soul of Matter.* Montpelier, VT: Invisible Cities, 2002.

de Zengotita, Thomas. *Mediated: How the Media Shapes Your World and the Way You Live in It.* New York: Bloomsbury Publishing, 2005.

Douglas, Susan. *Inventing American Broadcasting, 1899–1922.* Baltimore: Johns Hopkins University Press, 1987.

Douglas-Klotz, Neil. *The Sufi Book of Life.* New York: Penguin Compass, 2005.

Elgin, Duane. *Awakening Earth: Exploring the Evolution of Human Culture and Consciousness.* New York: William Morrow, 1993.

Fischer, Claude. *America Calling: A Social History of the Telephone to 1940.* Berkeley and Los Angeles: University of California Press, 1992.

Fox, Matthew. *Sins of the Spirit, Blessings of the Flesh: Lessons for Transforming Evil in Soul and Society.* New York: Harmony Books, 1999.

Goswami, Amit. *The Self-Aware Universe: How Consciousness Creates the Material World.* With Richard Reed and Maggie Goswami. Los Angeles: Jeremy P. Tarcher, 1993.

Grossinger, Richard. *On the Integration of Nature: Post 9/11 Biopolitical Notes.* Berkeley: North Atlantic Books, 2005.

Grosso, Michael. *The Millennium Myth: Love and Death at the End of Time*. Wheaton, IL: Theosophical Publishing House, Quest Books, 1997.

Hershock, Peter D. *Reinventing the Wheel: A Buddhist Response to the Information Age*. Albany: SUNY Press, 1999.

Johnson, Steven. *Everything Bad Is Good for You: How Today's Popular Culture Is Actually Making Us Smarter*. New York: Riverhead Books, 2005.

———. *Interface Culture: How New Technology Transforms the Way We Create and Communicate*. New York: HarperCollins, 1997.

Judith, Anodea. *Eastern Body Western Mind: Psychology and the Chakra System as a Path to Self*. Berkeley: Celestial Arts, 1996.

———. *Waking the Global Heart*. Santa Rosa, CA: Elite Books, 2006.

Judith, Anodea, and Selene Vega. *The Sevenfold Journey: Reclaiming Mind, Body and Spirit through the Chakras*. Freedom, CA: The Crossing Press, 1993.

Khan, Inayat. *The Heart of Sufism: Essential Writings*. Boston: Shambhala, 1999.

———. *The Sufi Message*. Vol. 5, *In an Eastern Rose Garden*. 2nd ed. Geneva: International Sufi Movement, 1979.

Khan, Vilayat Inayat. *Awakening: A Sufi Experience*. New York: Jeremy P. Tarcher, 1999.

———. *Toward the One*. New York: Harper Colophon, 1974.

Lasica, J. D. *Darknet: Hollywood's War Against the Digital Generation*. Hoboken, NJ: John Wiley & Sons, 2005.

Laszlo, Ervin. *Science and the Akashic Field: An Integral Theory of Everything*. Rochester, VT: Inner Traditions, 2004.

Levine, Fredrick, Christopher Locke, David (Doc) Searls, and David Weinberger. *The Cluetrain Manifesto: The End of Business as Usual*. Cambridge, MA: Perseus, 2000.

Levine, Stephen. *Turning Toward the Mystery*. New York: HarperCollins, 2002.

Levinson, Paul. *Cellphone: The Story of the World's Most Mobile Medium and How It Transformed Everything!* New York: Palgrave, 2004.

————. *The Soft Edge: A Natural History and Future of the Information Revolution*. New York: Routledge, 1997.

Lewis, Samuel. *Spiritual Dance and Walk*. San Francisco and Novato, CA: Sufi Islamia/Prophecy Publications, 1983.

Markoff, John. *What the Dormouse Said: How the Sixties Counterculture Shaped the Personal Computer Industry*. New York: Viking, 2005.

Maslow, Abraham. *Towards a Psychology of Being*. New York: Van Nostrand Reinhold, 1989.

Matt, Daniel C. *God and the Big Bang*. Woodstock VT: Jewish Lights, 1996.

McChesney, Robert W. *Telecommunications, Mass Media and Democracy: The Battle for the Control of U.S. Broadcasting, 1928–1935*. New York: Oxford University Press, 1993.

McKibben, Bill. *The Age of Missing Information*. New York: Random House, 1992.

McLuhan, Marshall. *Understanding Media: The Extensions of Man*. New York: McGraw Hill, 1964.

McTaggart, Lynn. *The Field*. U.S. edition. New York: HarperCollins, 2002.

Miller, Kempster, George Patterson, Charles Thom, Robert Millikan, and Samuel McMeen. *Cyclopedia of Telephony and Telegraphy*. Chicago: American School of Correspondence, 1919. Project Gutenberg E-Book no. 15617, April 2005, http://www.gutenberg.org/files/15617/15617-h/15617-h.htm.

Mosco, Vincent. *The Digital Sublime: Myth, Power and Cyberspace*. Cambridge, MA: MIT Press, 2004.

Mumford, Lewis. *Technics and Civilization*. New York: Harcourt, Brace & World, 1963.

Murphy, Michael. *The Future of the Body*. Los Angeles: Jeremy Tarcher, 1992.

Myss, Caroline. *Working With Your Chakras, Archetypes, and Sacred Contracts*. Carlsbad, CA: Hay House, 2001.

Nhat Hanh, Thich. *The Heart of Understanding: Commentaries on the Prajnaparamita Heart Sutra*. Berkeley: Parallax Press, 1988.

Ong, Walter J. *Orality and Literacy*. New York: Methuen and Co., 1987.

Pearce, Joseph Chilton. *Exploring the Crack in the Cosmic Egg*. New York: Julian Press, 1974.

Peters, John Durham. *Speaking Into the Air: A History of the Idea of Communications*. Chicago: The University of Chicago Press, 1999.

Pollan, Michael. *The Botany of Desire: A Plant's-Eye View of the World*. New York: Random House, 2001.

Ray, Paul, and Sherry Ruth Anderson. *The Cultural Creatives*. New York: Harmony Books, 2000.

Reynolds, Brad. *Where's Wilber At? Ken Wilber's Integral Vision in the New Millennium*. St. Paul, MN: Paragon House, 2006.

Rheingold, Howard. *Smart Mobs: The Next Social Revolution*. Cambridge, MA: Perseus, 2002.

————. *The Virtual Community: Homesteading on the Electronic Frontier*, 2nd ed. Cambridge: MIT Press, 2000.

Russell, Peter. *The Global Brain*. Los Angeles: Tarcher, 1983.

Satprem. *Sri Aurobindo, or The Adventure of Consciousness*. New York: Institute for Evolutionary Research, 1984.

Sconce, Jeffrey. *Haunted Media: Electronic Presence from Telegraphy to Television*. Durham, NC: Duke University Press, 2000.

Shlain, Leonard. *The Alphabet Versus the Goddess: The Conflict Between Word and Image*. New York: Viking-Penguin, 1998.

————. *Art and Physics: Parallel Visions of Space, Time and Light*. New York: William Morrow, 1991.

Shumsky, Susan G. *Exploring Chakras: Awaken Your Untapped Energy*. Franklin Lakes, NJ: New Page Books, 2003.

Standage, Tom. *The Victorian Internet: The Remarkable Story of the Telegraph and the 19th Century's On-Line Pioneers*. New York: Walker and Co., 1998.

Stark, Steven D. *Glued to the Set: The 60 Television Shows and Events That Made Us Who We Are Today*. New York: Free Press, 1997.

Stern, Ellen Stock, and Emily Gwathmey. *Once Upon a Telephone: An Illustrated Social History*. New York: Harcourt Brace and Company, 1994.

Talbot, Michael. *The Holographic Universe.* New York: Harper Collins, 1991.

Teilhard de Chardin, Pierre. *Let Me Explain.* Translated by René Hague. New York: Harper & Row, 1970.

———. *Man's Place in Nature.* Translated by René Hague. New York: Harper Colophon, 1966.

Thompson, William Irwin. *Coming into Being: Artifacts and Texts in the Evolution of Consciousness.* New York: St. Martin's Press, 1996.

Tolle, Eckhart. *Living the Liberated Life and Dealing with the Pain-Body.* Audio recording. Louisville, CO: Sounds True Audio, 2001.

———. *A New Earth: Awakening to Your Life's Purpose.* New York: Dutton/Penguin, 2005.

———. *The Power of Now.* Novato, CA: New World Library, 1999.

Wauters, Ambika. *Chakras and Their Archetypes: Uniting Energy Awareness and Spiritual Growth.* Freedom, CA: The Crossing Press, 1997.

Wedlake, G. E. C. *SOS: The Story of Radio Communications.* New York: Crane, Russak, 1973.

Wertheim, Margaret. *The Pearly Gates of Cyberspace.* New York: W. W. Norton, 1999.

White, John. *The Meeting of Science and Spirit.* New York: Paragon House, 1990.

Wilber, Ken. *The Atman Project: A Transpersonal View of Human Development.* Wheaton, IL: Theosophical Publishing House, Quest Books, 1980.

———. *A Brief History of Everything*, 2nd ed. Boston: Shambhala, 2002.

———. *Integral Psychology: Consciousness, Spirit, Psychology, Therapy.* Boston: Shambhala, 2000.

———. *The Spectrum of Consciousness.* Wheaton, IL: Theosophical Publishing House, Quest Books, 1977.

———. *A Theory of Everything.* Boston: Shambhala, 2000.

Winn, Marie. *The Plug-In Drug.* New York: Viking, 1985.

ILLUSTRATION CREDITS

Unless otherwise noted, illustrations are by Jennifer Hadley, Madison, Wisconsin.

Table 0.1 Technology images © www.clipart.com.

Fig. 1.2 Based on figure 15 in Miller et al., *Cyclopedia of Telephony and Telegraphy*.

Fig. 1.3 © 2007 www.clipart.com.

Fig. 2.1 © 2007 www.clipart.com.

Fig. 2.2 Used by permission of eShop Africa.

Fig. 2.3 Figure 296 in Miller et al., *Cyclopedia of Telephony and Telegraphy*.

Fig. 3.1 Courtesy of WHA Radio, University of Wisconsin-Madison Archives.

Fig. 3.2 © Groundswell Community Mural Project, 2005. Lead artist: Conor McGrady; youth artists: Kwabena "Cue" Johnson, Winston "Neo" Henry, Sergio Varel, Tiffany Joy, Melissa Torres, Issac Johnson.

Fig. 4.2 © Family Communications, Inc.

Fig. 6.1 © 2007 www.clipart.com.

Fig. 6.4 © 2007 Linden Research, Inc. All Rights Reserved.

Fig. 7.2 Courtesy of Thomas Fiedler, Berlin.

INDEX

Quest Books

encourages open-minded inquiry into
world religions, philosophy, science, and the arts
in order to understand the wisdom of the ages,
respect the unity of all life, and help people explore
individual spiritual self-transformation.

Its publications are generously supported by
The Kern Foundation,
a trust committed to Theosophical education.

Quest Books is the imprint of
the Theosophical Publishing House,
a division of the Theosophical Society in America.
For information about programs, literature,
on-line study, membership benefits, and international centers,
see www.theosophical.org
or call 800-669-1571 or (outside the U.S.) 630-668-1571.

To order books or a complete Quest catalog,
call 800-669-9425 or (outside the U.S.) 630-665-0130.

Praise for Steven Vedro's
DIGITAL DHARMA

"Exciting and engaging—a book that's been waiting to happen. Steven Vedro uses the language of information technology to describe the soul's journey or evolution (and vice versa). A very rich way to tell the ongoing human story, wherever it may be leading!"
—**Neil Douglas-Klotz, Ph.D.**, author of *The Genesis Meditations, The Hidden Gospel,* and *The Sufi Book of Life*

"Well done! You've pioneered a new aspect of noetic science."
—**John Warren White**, author of *The Meeting of Science and Spirit*

"Steven Vedro has written a fascinating book that intertwines the ancient wisdom of India with his consummate knowledge of the modern technology of information transfer. Comparing the various chakras with the history of human communication, he presents startlingly fresh insights into the connection between the world of technological advances and a more fundamental ground of being. A compelling read."
—**Leonard Shlain**, author of *The Alphabet Versus the Goddess*

"Steven Vedro's insights are too important to go unnoticed, especially in these times when most trends in mass media are *away* from humanistic and spiritual values. We need visionaries like him to draw our attention to the difference between information and wisdom, and to the relationship between the digital and the divine. Bravo!"
—**Christian de Quincey, Ph.D.,** cofounder, The Visionary Edge; Professor of Philosophy and Conscious Studies, John F. Kennedy University; author of *Radical Nature* and *Radical Knowing*

"Digital Dharma is an excellent portrayal of the history and near future of telecommunications."
—**Peter Russell,** author of *From Science to God* and *The Global Brain Awakens*

"Whether you read it as metaphor or metaphysics, *Digital Dharma* is an ingenious exploration of the hidden links between communications technology and the human psyche. Vedro knows his stuff about media and the mysteries, but he writes as a peer, not a guru. Tune in and turn on."
—**Erik Davis**, author of *TechGnosis* and *The Visionary State*